I made the mistake of reading the ... restaurant, which resulted in a hero... a deluge of tears. After all, men do ... Christian men don't write books abo... Well, James Carroll just did and the ... ...autifully sensitive and moving Gospel-biography that even his parents have supported. Yes, you will shed tears of sorrow over the pain of sin and its agonizing consequences. But you will also shed tears of joy over the healing power of Christ and the astonishing love of God's people for a heart-broken 12-year-old boy.

David Murray,
Pastor, Grand Rapids Free Church and Professor of Old Testament
and Practical Theology, Puritan Reformed Seminary
Grand Rapids, Michigan

In his first book, *Collateral Damage*, Dr. James Carroll has lifted the veil on one of the more painful and, frankly, humiliating events that has permanently marked his life and his family of origin. In so doing, Carroll, with his parents' permission, has given an invaluable gift to the church. How can the church love a family in crisis? What if that family is the pastor's family? Carroll shares his personal journey and communicates how the balm of the gospel becomes the primary source of care and healing for every soul. As a product of a broken family myself, and a fellow recipient of God's grace showered upon me by the loving care of my church family, I can testify to the truth and power of Carroll's testimony and exhortation. Every soul is broken by personal sin and the consequences of others' sin and every Christian is called to minister to broken souls, beginning with his or her own. Carroll's book is a consecrated prescription to follow.

Paul Chitwood
Executive Director-Treasurer, Kentucky Baptist Convention
Louisville, Kentucky

James Carroll is a gifted communicator, both verbally and in writing. I read this book with great anticipation believing it would help me be a better minister. It already has and will continue to do so. Carroll's paradigm of breaking down pastoral care with hurting people into holistic care, immediate care, intensive care, and long-term care is incredibly helpful. But this book also challenged and encouraged me personally. His insights into our tendencies toward self-pity and self-righteousness are worth the price of the book alone. Our brokenness doesn't need to mirror what Carroll experienced for this book to be life-changing. This work is solid gold. Buy it. Read it. Apply it. You and those around you will be glad you did.

Timothy K. Beougher
Billy Graham Professor of Evangelism and Associate Dean of the
Billy Graham School of Missions, Evangelism and Ministry
The Southern Baptist Theological Seminary, Louisville, Kentucky

Redemption. Rescue. Restoration. These are the words that came to the forefront of my mind as I read this painful, yet hope-filled account of God's work of transforming a 12-year old Pharisee into a humble, imperfect pastor. This little book is sober, yet gentle as a warning to pastors and fathers. Nevertheless, it also overflows with grace as we hear another testimony of the gospel's power to rescue each of us from our sin in order to magnify God's glory through earthen vessels.

Paul Tautges
Senior Pastor, Cornerstone Community Church, Cleveland, Ohio
and Author, *Comfort the Grieving*

When a pastor like James Carroll offers counsel on care for the sufferers, you listen. When you realize that James himself has suffered, you really listen! Here's a book that proves 2 Cor 1:4; our hardships hold in store serious ministry potential. Heart-wrenchingly honest and immensely helpful all at the same time.

Liam Garvie
Associate Pastor
Charlotte Chapel, Edinburgh, Scotland

COLLATERAL DAMAGE

MY JOURNEY TO HEALING FROM MY PASTOR AND FATHER'S FAILURE

JAMES B. CARROLL

AFTERWORD BY CHRIS CARROLL

CHRISTIAN
FOCUS

Practical
Shepherding

Copyright © James B. Carroll 2017
paperback 978-1-5271-0003-9
epub 978-1-5271-0033-6
mobi 978-1-5271-0034-3

First published in 2017
by
Christian Focus Publications Ltd,
Geanies House, Fearn, Ross-shire,
IV20 1TW, Scotland.

www.christianfocus.com

with

Practical Shepherding, Inc
P.O. Box 21806
Louisville, Kentucky 40221, USA

www.practicalshepherding.com

A CIP catalogue record for this book is available from the British Library.

Cover design by Moose77.com

Printed and bound by
Bell and Bain, Glasgow

Contents

To my mom (Toni), my dad (Chris),
and my brother (Mark).

God blessed me by placing me in your family.
I wouldn't trade any of you for another. I pray these
pages bring healing to each of you. I love you.

Foreword
Brian Croft

Her story was heartbreaking. It started as I sat conducting a membership interview with Tammy and John. This middle-aged couple had moved into the area and had found a home in our local church. As part of the membership process I met with them to hear their stories. I began to hear details about Tammy's life that were both disturbing and tragic. She was a pastor's kid; her father was a pastor throughout her entire upbringing. But it was not the warm experience one would hope.

Tammy shared that her father was a manipulative, domineering tyrant who was abusive to her and all her siblings. She shared a story where her father during his sermon verbally attacked her and her siblings in front of the whole church when they had not obeyed one of his instructions. This apparently was common practice. You can imagine this type of behavior in a church was not received well, so her family moved around a lot as her father went from church to church. This man's poisonous demeanor was brought into the home, where Tammy reflected on the fear the whole family deeply held towards him, and on the confusion about God this brought each sibling, in their own unique way.

Reflecting back on those years Tammy, now in her forties, shared about the consequences of such an upbringing in a pastor's home. With tears, she told of her brother and sister addicted to drugs and alcohol, who were in and out of rehab., and many suicide attempts of another sibling. Every sibling was either on multiple marriages, or married to abusive spouses where horrible dysfunction and family turmoil was the norm. And yet, here sat Tammy – with a different story.

Married only once, to a man who held her hand as she shared this painful account of her family, it was clear Tammy was a person who dearly loved Jesus and was following Him. She was a woman who did not hold bitterness and anger to God for this family life, but went to Him for comfort in the pain of it. She loved the church and wanted to join ours, desiring a pastor's care for her soul.

As I listened to her story, I had tears in my eyes for two reasons. First, I felt deep sorrow over the pain her father/ pastor caused her and her family all those years, and how that manifested in her siblings' adult lives. As a pastor myself, I uniquely felt the weight of what is at stake for my own family. Second, I was amazed that she had not experienced the same devastation to her life as her siblings. She should have. It is appropriate to ask, 'Why?' Why was this woman not angry at God? Why would she even want anything to do with Jesus and the church? How could she trust in any way another pastor and man to care for her soul? There is only one answer: God's grace. Because God's grace was so powerfully evident in this woman's life, I realized she carried a wisdom and perspective about life that is worth special consideration.

This book contains another tragic story of a pastor's family devastated by sin. It is written by an author who experienced it firsthand. Because of the devastating effects a pastor's sin can have on his family, this author too should hate God, want nothing to do with Jesus or His church, and be acting out the patterns of sin that he witnessed. But this book is not written by such a man. By God's grace, James is different. He loves the church; he exudes love and forgiveness towards his father (as you will read). He even loves pastors; he too is a pastor. Like Tammy, by God's amazing grace this man also has a special and unique wisdom and perspective on life, ministry, and the challenges of the pastor's family that should be carefully considered.

This book is his story. In it, Pastor James Carroll gives tangible evidence of how the power of God's grace in the gospel of Jesus Christ took the heartbreak of a twelve-year-old boy and transformed him into a strong, wise, and compassionate minister of the gospel, and shepherd of God's people. Because of this redemptive journey, James has powerful insights into local church life and how a church can care well for both the pastor's family as well as hurting members. Read this moving story. Learn the valuable lessons that will transform how you care for your pastor as well as the hurting people in your church. Most of all, marvel at the grace of God and how God redeems the most tragic and heartbreaking moments of our lives for our good and His glory.

BRIAN CROFT
Senior Pastor, Auburndale Baptist Church,
Founder, Practical Shepherding.

May 2016

Introduction
That's Gonna Leave a Mark

Many of my early memories are connected to church life as a pastor's son. My dad served as pastor of Southern Baptist churches deep in the Bible-belt culture of rural Kentucky for several years. These small communities of faith remained somewhat insulated from the secular influences making inroads upon larger culture in the 1980s. Even as a public school kid who played sports in the community, I was somewhat safely cocooned in a Christian culture. It was warm and snuggly in there and I liked it.

I wore a little clip-on tie to church, standing with my dad at the back door to greet exiting worshipers. I carried my Bible, prided myself on dominating Bible drills, and tagged along for home visits and attended funerals. I knew the standard hymns by heart, and told a wide variety of preacher jokes. I knew when to bow, when to stand, when to sing, and when to be quiet. I wasn't perfect, but knew how to play the part. And I rather enjoyed it.

Then one night, it all ended.

My parents separated a few weeks before I started seventh grade. Unbeknownst to me, the trouble in our home had been brewing for a long time. Their divorce wouldn't become final for months, but the initial damage to my world was complete within a few days. Our family fractured, my dad lost his job, and my identity evaporated in a flash.

The purpose of this book is neither to rehash what led to my parents' divorce nor to condemn twenty-five-year-old sins. Instead, I want to walk through my experience of suffering and maturing through another person's sin. Divorce always involves sin. I did not participate in it, but I suffered as a result of it. To borrow a familiar phrase, I was collateral damage: I was the passenger in a family barreling down life's road. We careened off the road and broke into pieces. The scene wasn't pretty and we were all injured. But God remained faithful.

I love my parents deeply and respect them both. My parents have taught me much about what it means to follow Christ and have impacted my life spiritually in more ways than anyone else. The last thing I want to do is disparage or disrespect either of them. For months in contemplating and then writing the book, I've wrestled with how to share this story without dishonoring my parents. God is glorified in this story, so I want to tell it. I'm also keenly aware that in Christ, the fifth commandment applies to my mouth and my keyboard. However, God's grace to me wasn't vague. He didn't restore in abstract ways, or heal nebulous wounds ambiguously; He was specific. He mended brokenness, removed bitterness, revealed my sins, confronted my pride, and drew me closer to Himself. He sanctified me. And I can't describe the wounds and the healing without taking you back to the scene of the accident. So here goes.

Looking back I could see that the wheels were starting to come off for several months. Odd behaviors and increased tension in the home made me wonder what was happening. But from inside the cocoon, I kept telling myself everything was normal. Then on a Wednesday night in the summer of 1989, it all came crashing down. As I recall, we arrived home at different times, which wasn't unusual. We lived fifty yards from the church building in the parsonage so we walked to and from most church meetings. Because of the nature of our evening meetings, we rarely came home together. That night, after we had all made it home, my parents gathered my brother Mark and me for a family talk. Let's pause on that story however. In order to appreciate the devastation of that night, I need to take you back a little further; six years earlier to be exact.

In the summer of 1983, I distinctly recall us gathering as a family on a Wednesday evening. We lived in a similarly-placed parsonage next to a different church building in another part of rural Kentucky, where my dad served as pastor. We gathered in the kitchen because I had an announcement to share with the family. While the adults held the weekly prayer meeting earlier that evening, I participated in the children's ministry activities in the basement of that little country-church building. I don't remember anything about the activities that night: not the lesson nor the songs nor the snack (if they even gave us one). But I remember vividly that as they concluded the Bible lesson, they asked if anyone wanted to be saved. I remember raising my hand, sitting with an adult leader (whose name and face I can't remember), walking through a gospel tract and asking God to save me.

My profession of faith and prayer of repentance wasn't the beginning of that story. In the months leading up to responding to the gospel, I had sat on my dad's lap numerous times in his office talking about God, about my sin, and about Jesus' life, death, and resurrection. I remember my mom singing about and sharing the good news of Jesus in our home and in the car. While I wasn't ready to write a treatise on justification by faith, I understood the good news and I trusted in Jesus. So that night, in the single-wide trailer, among tobacco and cattle farms of central Kentucky, across from the little white church building, our family of four celebrated. I don't remember every detail, but that little kitchen was full of smiles of thanksgiving, tears of joy, and hearts of hope. God was faithful, and had come to save. He overcame sin and brought new life.

Now back to 1989. The tone this time of the family gathering was somber and tense. My dad had resigned as pastor that night and we would be moving soon. The whole conversation was strange from the beginning. While my parents protected us from many aspects of church life, we were always invited into the prayer and conversations when they were considering ministry transitions. But the abruptness of this decision was vastly different from all the rest. This time the resignation was necessary and future ministry was on hold. They spared us many details, but we heard enough. My dad's affections wandered outside our home. He had attached himself emotionally to another woman; crossing the line, his heart was entangled. At the time questions like when, why, how, and whom seemed to matter, but ultimately, they didn't. And they don't. The mood in our home that Wednesday night in 1989 stood in stark contrast to the mood on the Wednesday six years earlier. There were no smiles. The tears were born out of grief and sadness; our hearts were full of anxiety and despair.

That massive fracture opened the floodgates, but there had been smaller fissures along the way. I don't know all of them and I don't want to. What I do know is that sin doesn't usually start big; it starts small and becomes big. I know that marriages don't often end because of a single disastrous moment. Even when a jarring crash is the death knell, the sin grows inconspicuously for a while.

The next few days were like riding in the Tea Cups at Disney World. It's the ride where you sit in a circle inside a big cup and spin while it moves chaotically along with other cups on the big track. The world spun around-and-around while my head was trying to keep up. My stomach was upside-down and in knots, but I didn't feel like vomiting. I could hear laughter in the background because life was still going on as usual for everyone else, but I didn't feel like being part of it. Even now, it's bizarre to think about those days.

Despite a few promising moments (at least in the eyes of a twelve-year-old), in the next few days the damage was irreparable. What was broken would never be put back as it once was. My dad relocated quickly, leaving my mom, my brother, and me living in that church parsonage. No one had a firm plan for the future; we were all reeling. But God was still faithful, who is the same, yesterday, today, and forever. And His faithfulness didn't bend or flex once. God remained there, still saving. In 1983, He had rescued me from His wrath that resulted from my sin: In 1989 and the years following, He kept on rescuing me from the spiritual and emotional wounds from my sin and the sins of other people.

After more than a dozen years in pastoral ministry, I know my life circumstances are unique *and* common. No one else can tell my story. You weren't in those parsonages on those Wednesday evenings; you didn't experience suffering because of sin in my family. But everyone has a story like mine. Every one of us suffers because of sin we do not commit. Sometimes we suffer as an indirect result of sin. Tornadoes and tumors are not caused by a person's specific sins, but they bring destruction because sin taints the world. From the mild aggravation of poison ivy to the devastation of inoperable cancer, we are suffering because this world groans as a result of Adam's sin. We now live in a world riddled with the consequences of sin.

Yet the suffering isn't only indirect. Other times, as what I'm describing in my life, also come as a direct result of another person's sin; every one of us suffers in this way. In these times Adam's sin is still the root cause, but there is a closer, more direct cause. The consequences are derived from a spouse, a parent, a sibling, a child, a friend, or an enemy: he hit me; she stole from me; he gossiped about me; she cheated.

So while the details of my story are unique, the story is actually quite common. These injuries come in different shapes and sizes. Some people bear obvious scars from their emotional, mental, and spiritual wounds. Some conceal the hurt by suppressing or even denying it. Still others live at risk, not realizing they're wounded. So how can we respond? It's this question that spurs me to write.

In these pages, I share my story and some lessons I've learned along the way. While I pray these lessons will encourage readers who are suffering now, my more direct aim is to equip pastors and church leaders for ministering well to those who suffer. Every situation is different, so you won't find a textbook or how-to guide for this type of care here. Instead, I'll walk you through my experience and share wisdom and insight. In short, I want to shine light on the glory of God in the gospel of Jesus. This gospel is the power of God to save, to restore, and to heal. He promised it and He is faithful. Because He is faithful, we can minister with hope and joy to those who are wounded by sin and languishing in despair. We can come alongside those who are mangled by the consequences of sin and point them toward Christ, because He is our hope.

The plan is to carry the metaphor of trauma forward to describe four types of care involved in ministering to the wounded. In part one, I'll zoom all the way out to see that the gospel is the only solution, and the Bible is the primary tool for explaining and applying these truths to those who are hurting. In the second part, I will reflect upon two of the immediate and most important instruments for this ministry. After the dust of a sin's initial consequence has settled, this ministry evolves into intense discipleship. I will explain dual aspects of this intensive care in part three. I'll close in part four with a reminder that gospel ministry doesn't end until we meet Christ face-to-face.

So I was a broken, wounded, and reeling twelve-year-old boy. My cocoon was gone. My family was fractured. But by God's grace that's not the end of my story; it's only the beginning. Following that dreadful Wednesday night, a beautiful, but crooked journey to healing in the gospel-saturated context of a community of faith began to emerge.

Part I.
Holistic Care

1.
The Gospel is the Remedy

I am not now, nor have I ever been, particularly handy. Given a reasonable amount of time and the proper tools, I can usually figure out how something works and fumble toward a solution. But I am not naturally inclined or gifted to fix things, especially those of the mechanical variety. My attempts at home and at auto repair usually lead to bigger messes, requiring twice as much time and energy than was originally needed. I'll give you an example.

Several years ago I repaired my Ford F-150 pickup truck. It wouldn't start; I replaced a part, and it started working again. While I'm sure it's a gross oversimplification, I figured my truck's problem had to be located in one of two areas: power or ignition. Either the engine wasn't getting the proper power or it lacked initial combustion. Because of my financial limitations, I decided to have a look under the hood.

I knew to look for two potential problems: a dead battery and a bad starter solenoid. While checking the battery was obvious, I only knew about the solenoid because I had watched a friend make repairs to one in the past. To this day, it's the only part I have ever replaced under the hood of any automobile (I have replaced head lights that I accessed under the hood, but not even I will act as though that constitutes automotive repair).

After a quick look at my F-150, I determined that everything seemed to be in the factory-specified location. Even more, the battery didn't appear to be my problem. So I tried a little trick I'd been taught to test the solenoid. For any novice readers, the solenoid is sometimes called the starter relay and its job is to manage two electric currents that allow a car to start. When you turn the key, it receives a small electric current from the ignition and then relays the large current from the car battery to start the motor, which sets the engine in motion. Lost yet? Sorry. I didn't know all of that at the time either.

Here's what I knew. There is a $20 part bolted to the frame under the hood not far from the windshield wipers. If it goes bad, the car won't start. Protruding from it are two bolts and you can check to see if it's your problem by touching both at the same time with a screwdriver and trying to start the engine. If it cranks when you 'bypass' the solenoid using the screwdriver, it's your problem. Well, I had a friend who was brave (or stupid) enough to hold the screwdriver for me so I gave it a try. The truck engine started. At that point I decided I could fix it.

I drove to the auto-part store, explained what I needed, bought my part, and headed home. I removed the old one, compared it to the new one, and realized my next problem. Apparently, make, model, *and* engine size are all important when buying a solenoid. So I returned to the auto-part store and traded the part in for the correct one, then began installing the solenoid. Remember the two bolts? Once the part is bolted to the frame (which was no easy task for me), one cable is fastened to each of these bolts. One cable comes from the battery and the other from the ignition. As I'm tightening the nut on the last bolt I realize that it's turning more than the other. Instead of stopping to examine things more closely, I just kept cranking away until … snap! In my inexperience, I had over-tightened the nut and snapped the bolt off the front of the solenoid. There I stood holding the broken pieces of my own attempts at car repair, frustrated, embarrassed, and worse off than when I'd started.

Does this sound familiar? I didn't break the solenoid originally, but I was convinced I could fix it. I can laugh about it now, but as a twelve-year-old kid, I was convinced I could fix my parents and heal our family. Youthful exuberance and naiveté aside, I was completely ignorant of the spiritual reality of our situation. My parents needed the gospel. Other books, really good books, have been written about their need and how the gospel is applied to people in the midst of their sinful trauma.

I'm writing, though, because I also needed the gospel. I was the victim of the consequences of their sin and it was the gospel I needed. Yes, I had trusted in Jesus for salvation and had been saved from the penalty of sin. But the gospel is also the power of God to free us from the power of sin. He keeps working to transform and keep us until the end. Through the gospel, God dispenses grace to heal and restore. This includes the obvious healing of our fracture with Him because of our sin. Through the gospel, He establishes a right relationship with us and extends grace to heal us from the ongoing fractures caused by our sin and by that of others.

Rightly applied, the gospel reorients us and shapes our worldview by becoming the proper lens through which we understand the world. And when wounded by someone else's sin, the gospel brings the grace and truth again needed to heal and reorient. The gospel was the remedy for my situation. In simplest terms, this book is the story of how God over and over applied the gospel to me. So before we see how God used the gospel in more detail, let's review what it is.

The gospel is the message of God's plan and His work to save sinners from His wrath, and to bring them into a relationship with Himself through the work of Jesus Christ, and the offer of that rescue to all who will turn from sin and trust in Christ.

I've used this 'definition' for several years and I can't recall all the places I've borrowed from to get it where it is. Nothing in it is new, but I don't remember copying it verbatim from any one place. It is a very pregnant sentence and it demands unpacking.

First and obviously, the *gospel* is a message or definitive collection of concepts that relate a specific, joyous announcement. In other words, it has a singular definition. Unfortunately, in some circles the gospel has become something of a moving target that bends and flexes as we roam along from culture to culture and society to society. However, biblical revelation provides one definition. The gospel is a specific story, and it is a happy story. In fact, it's often called the good news because it tells a distinct and glad story. Thus, the power of God through the gospel comes only when a person has heard and understood this specific message.

Second, the *gospel* relates 'God's plan and His work'. This message begins with God. He is the holy, righteous Creator. He is eternal (meaning He exists before all things) and He is transcendent (meaning He is above and beyond all things). The gospel is *His* story. It's the one narrative He's been unfolding from the foundation of the world. God is not reacting to man's whims or figuring it out as He goes along. God is working out His sovereign and meticulous plan. In the gospel this plan is announced. Otherwise, we'd never know about it. But the gospel isn't merely about the plan; it also tells of God's work. God is the Actor; He is not a mere bystander. God doesn't direct affairs from afar; He works to accomplish His plan and to reveal it.

Third, the *gospel* tells of 'God's plan and His work to save sinners'. He is not simply making moral people or helping people find their purpose in life. God is first of all rescuing men and women from the penalty and power of sin. People are drowning in the lake of their rebellion against God and He is reaching into the water to 'save' them. As Jesus said, 'For I came not to call the righteous, but sinners' (Matt. 9:13b). According to this story, every person born on the earth has inherited a will inclined to sin and all people willingly join in rebellion against God. From our earliest days, we shake our fists at our Creator, seeking to usurp control of our own lives. The gospel makes a strong statement about mankind: namely, we are sinners and we stand in desperate need of rescue from our sin and its consequence.

Fourth, the *gospel* offers salvation from 'His wrath'. The consequence of our rebellion is the wrath of God. This is best understood as His settled reaction toward sin. Unlike human wrath, God's wrath is never out of control, never lacks wisdom, and is never cool or indifferent. God's wrath is His directed, intense, just reaction to sin. It is not an impulsive flying off the handle, fit of rage.

The practical result of this wrath is death. We die physically as we pay the penalty for our sin. But we also die spiritually as we pay the penalty for our sin. The Bible describes this spiritual death as separation from God. The agony of this separation will reach its highest (or we might say lowest) point when God judges all people and brings everlasting punishment upon those men and women who have continued in their rebellion. The Bible calls the place where these people will suffer for eternity hell and describes it as a lake of unquenchable fire. So, the gospel is the message of God's work to rescue or save people from His wrath, which they justly deserve because of sin.

Fifth, the *gospel* tells of God's work to bring sinners into a right 'relationship with Himself'. Isaiah 59:2 makes a clear and alarming proclamation about sin and its effect on a person's relationship to God:

> but your iniquities have made a separation
>   between you and your God,
> and your sins have hidden his face from you
>   so that he does not hear.

As sinners, we sit hopelessly under His wrath which separates us from Him. Despite His great love for us, He will not and He cannot overlook our sin and tarnish His perfection and justice. The gospel, though, is the story of how God crossed this chasm created by our sin and is bringing sinners back to Himself.

Sixth, the *gospel* tells of the 'work of Jesus Christ'. God's work to save was accomplished through the life, death, and resurrection of Jesus. He is the only Son of the Father and a full member of the Godhead. Yet, He donned flesh and lived as a human being, providing the only way to salvation. Thus, this good story centers on Jesus and His work. Through His human life, Jesus condescends to our level while satisfying God's standard perfectly. Not deserving death, He dies sacrificially in the place of others, bearing God's wrath for them and making atonement for their sin. He died our death, but He could not be held by death. God raised Him from the dead, announcing victory over sin and death, and foreshadowing the full and final statement of victory that is coming.

Seventh, the *gospel* story tells of what has happened, but it doesn't stop there. This story includes an invitation. Its message announces the solution to the deepest problem in our soul (our separation from God because of our sin) and it holds out the offer of the gift of forgiveness and eternal life. This gift comes only by grace, which is God's unmerited favor towards us. This gift, however, must be received by faith.

Eighth, the *gospel* invites a person to trust in Jesus for salvation. This faith is not mental assent. Instead, it's best understood as a heart-response of repentance from sin and surrender to Christ. Repentance is a change of mind resulting in a turn from sin. To receive the gospel a person must submit to God reorienting their will away from sin. However, do not misunderstand repentance as work or merit. Rather it is a heart-level hatred for sin that comes as a reaction inside a person who hears the gospel and trusts in Jesus.

Again, this faith produces a surrender of allegiance to Christ as King and Ruler. Faith in Jesus is life-altering, causing us to rely solely on His work to deal with our sin, and to yield absolutely to follow Him at any cost. This active faith is the means by which God appropriates salvation. The work of Jesus to cover our sin and to re-establish our relationship with God is only applied to persons who trust fully in Him. When a person places his faith in Jesus, God applies His work to that person and saves him from sin and its eternal consequences.

By God's wisdom and providence, He uses the proclamation of this gospel to draw people to a faith that sets them free from His wrath. Romans 10:17 states most clearly the wonderful promise, 'So faith comes from hearing, and hearing through the word of Christ.' So we preach this gospel because, by it, people believe and are saved.

This story of rescue from sin provides the context for my story and the solution to my hurt. This story changed my life as an almost six-year-old boy when, after hearing it over and over from my parents and others, I trusted in Jesus for salvation. But it's been even more than that. This story has been the instrument of God to heal my hurt, lead me to forgive, restore my relationship to my parents, and help my faith persevere.

God used good friends, wise counsel, and faithful prayers as instruments of grace in my life, but the gospel is His power to save, restore, and heal. So there I was in the summer of 1989: frustrated, embarrassed, and staring at the broken pieces of my life. I sure wish my life could be repaired as easily as a solenoid starter on an F-150. But my journey to healing is actually much more beautiful. I had no idea how desperately I needed the gospel. Thankfully, I wasn't alone and God wasn't finished.

2.
The Bible is the Textbook

Have you ever tried to convince someone of something they already believe? I've felt that way as a preacher. I'm engrossed in persuasion, zealously pounding away about some aspect of theology, while most of the congregation listens politely. They seem to be thinking, 'I already knew that Jesus is God's Son, but thank you.'

Worse still is trying to convince someone of something they *think* they believe, but probably don't. If you're an evangelical Christian reading this book, you'll be tempted to skim through this chapter because you're convinced it's for someone else. Please be careful, though: this is vitally important. Most of us say we believe the Bible is God's word, but I'm not sure we do.

The Bible is the Word of God. The sixty-six books of the Old and New Testaments are God's Word given in human words. Gordon Fee explains: 'The Bible holds two realities in tension: eternal relevance and historical particularity.' Eternal relevance means it speaks to all people in every age and in every culture. Historical particularity means that each document is conditioned by the language, time, and culture in which it was originally written.[1]

The Bible is the living, active word of the living God. It was written by men but authored by God through divine inspiration. The Bible is God's special, self-revelation to man. If we want to know God – either His character or His will – we must turn first to the Bible, as it is the place He can most certainly be found. I've been helped by T. H. L. Parker's statement about the Bible:

> The Scriptures are not man's guesses about the mystery of God, nor are they the conclusions that men have drawn from certain data at their disposal. On the contrary, they are the unveiling of the mystery of God by God Himself – God's gracious revelation of Himself to ignorant and sinful men.[2]

The Bible is inerrant – meaning without error – and reliable; it is trustworthy and true. David Dockery helpfully clarifies:

---

1. Gordon D. Fee and Douglas Stuart, *How to Read the Bible for All It's Worth* (Grand Rapids: Zondervan, 2003), p. 21.

2. T. H. L. Parker, *Portrait of Calvin* (Minneapolis. MN: Desiring God, 2009), EPUB, p. 62.

> When all the facts are known, the Bible (in its original writings), properly interpreted in light of which culture and communication means had developed by the time of its composition will be shown to be completely true (and therefore not false) in all that it affirms, to the degree of precision intended by the author, in all matters relating to God and his creation.[3]

Even more, the Bible is the source for divine instruction and the absolute authority concerning issues of faith and practice. Regarding those issues to which the Bible speaks directly and clearly, we must seek to listen, understand, and obey. Concerning those issues to which the Bible speaks indirectly or less clearly, we must seek to understand all related biblical texts and discern the truth, leaning on the Holy Spirit for guidance.

Therefore, the Bible is the authority under which we understand who God is and how we are to live in the world He created. Everything in the Bible is true and trustworthy, but it doesn't contain all truths that *can* be known. In other words, there are true statements that are not in the Bible. Yet, it contains everything necessary for spiritual growth and godliness. For every spiritual need that may arise, the Bible contains the solution. It is sufficient for us to know God and know how to live for Him.

In fact, it's even simpler than that. The gospel is the heart of every solution. Further, the Bible contains sufficient information about how the gospel is applied to every

---

3. David S. Dockery, *Christian Scripture: An Evangelical Perspective on Inspiration, Authority, and Interpretation* (Eugene, OR: Wipf & Stock, 2004), p. 64.

situation. No matter what the context – strained marriage, terminal illness, stressful job, financial crisis, rebellious child, drug addiction, fierce opposition, intense persecution, sexual abuse, divorce, or tragic loss – the Bible equips us to endure and even grow in Christ. Books can be very helpful. I mean, I'm investing all these hours to write one, for goodness sake. But this book will only foster healing in your life in proportion to my ability to capture the truth of God's word, explain it, and uncover its application to life situations. The Bible alone is sufficient to cultivate spiritual transformation.

I am convinced, though, that despite our immediate agreement with this truth, most evangelical Christians don't really believe it. On the most practical level, we turn everywhere except the Bible. Some feel they must look elsewhere out of necessity because the Bible doesn't say everything. Let me illustrate.

Newton's Third Law of Motion is commonly explained by the sentence, 'For every action there is an equal, but opposite reaction.' But did you know that most airplanes create propulsion or thrust using a jet engine that is built on this law? Even more, do you know why a fixed-wing aircraft that is propelled at a particularly high rate of speed lifts off the ground? This lift is a result of the pressure differences created by the swiftly-moving aircraft cutting through the force of the air that is resting on itself and on the earth. I didn't know it and I'll bet very few of you did. But if you're going to travel around the world in an airplane, somebody better know these things. These are important facts for air travel, but they are not recorded in the Bible.

The earth is spherical in shape. The human body contains trillions of cells. A proper sentence must have subject-verb agreement. For a plant to grow, it needs water, sunlight, and nutrients from the soil. What goes up must come down. We could list facts for hours. The Bible contains so much information, but it doesn't contain every factual statement about our world or even our bodies. Herein lies the point we – and by 'we' I mean Bible-believing followers of Jesus – often veer off track when it comes to the Bible. We are confident in what the Bible says; we just don't think it says enough.

Adultery and divorce are sin. They are outside God's design for marriage and, as such, they are an assault on God and His holiness. They are also the fruit of an inner rebellion against God. Like all sin, they separate us from God and place us under His wrath. Unless we find forgiveness of sin through Jesus, we will perish because of these sins. I know this because the Bible tells me: it is so helpful in answering eternal questions.

But adultery and divorce are not just eternal problems. Certainly, they bring the wrath of God, but they also destroy families. A twelve-year-old boy living in a household broken apart by them is unmistakably shaken and shaped by it. He's not facing the wrath of God because of them; instead, he's facing a range of emotions he doesn't understand and can't process. The boy is filled with sadness, insecurity, anger, anxiety, and despair, while at the same time, he doesn't really care what mom and dad are fighting about because he wants to play video games. He's more concerned with who's taking him to basketball practice than the spiritual dimension of the warfare that recently broke out in his home.

So where is a young boy to turn? How can we help him cope with the trauma? I sure wish somebody would write a book about that. This is because the Bible can tell him how to be forgiven of his sin, inform him how to do what Jesus wants, and fill his head with facts about God, but it doesn't say everything. He doesn't need to know that Jesus died to pay the penalty for his parents' sin. Or does he? The Bible won't tell you how to walk a young boy through this situation any more than it will tell you how to fly a plane. Or will it? A baseline assumption of this book is that the Bible is sufficient for this work.

At twelve years old, I could flatly dominate a Bible-drill. 'Attention.' 'Present Bibles.' 'Fill in the blank with any reference.' I didn't need a table of contents, and the thumb index editions were for lightweights or cheaters. Just give me a hardback, King-James-Version, pew Bible and let's roll. I knew Jude only had one chapter and I could navigate the Minor Prophets. I was far from cool, but I was church-camp cool. I knew the Bible about as well as a kid could know it, but I had no idea how it could help when my world became unglued.

From this point forward in my story, therefore, I want to make something clear. The Bible is not an abstract fact-book. It is a source of life-giving nourishment, sufficient to meet our spiritual need. Wait. There's just one more problem. This nourishment is more like a vitamin than a steroid.

Our church recently installed an electronic check in system for our children and pre-school ministries. The new system adds new levels of security and efficiency. After only a few weeks, we traded in our first set of label printers for a second set because of some technological issues. The best part of the upgrade was that the new printers actually worked. Coming in a close second is that they print the labels in less than half the time. The speed for printing my family's three labels has now been reduced from a molasses-like twenty-eight seconds to a lightning-esque ten seconds. Amazing!

Do you realize how much life I'll have back now? If I check in my children 125 times a year, that's more than 1,700 seconds I can recoup – almost thirty minutes a year. Do you realize how many more meaningful conversations I can have with members of our family of faith because I won't be staring blankly at the printer for fifteen extra seconds? Ministry will improve; new relationships forged; transformation spawned. I think I'll be a much better pastor now. It's really about stewardship of resources and especially time: I'm not so much impatient as that I am committed to efficiency.

This sounds silly even as I type it. Again I'm impatient, and I know it. If we're honest, we all are, and we bring these expectations to the Bible.

It often goes something like this. I've got five minutes this morning for a quiet time. Where can I turn for encouragement and motivation? I'll read a psalm. Um, let's see: my birthday is on the seventh day of the month so I'll try Psalm 7!

Verse 1: '*in you do I take refuge ... save me from all my pursuers ...* . So far, so good. Verse 3: '*If I have done ... wrong ... .*' Okay, a little confession; I can handle that. Verse 5: '*let the enemy ... trample my life to the ground ... .*' Whoa, hold on a minute. This is not going the way

I planned; but keep reading. Verse 11: *'a God who feels indignation every day.'* Really? Verse 12: *'God will whet his sword ... .'* Verse 13, *'He has prepared ... deadly weapons ... .'* Yikes, that sounds harsh. Verse 17: *'I will give to the Lord the thanks due his righteousness, and I will sing praise to the name of the Lord, the Most High.'* Okay, good save. I guess that song was encouraging for David when he wrote it. And if I was fighting a war today, I bet that picture of God as the righteous warrior would seem pretty powerful. But I really expected a boost for today and I didn't quite get it.

So goes the approach to the Bible for many of us. Yes, I did put *us*. Pastors are tempted to do the same thing. But God's word works differently in us. He saturates us with the truth over and over, slowly bending our hearts and shaping our minds. A shot here and there won't do; we must drink from this fountain slowly over the course of time.

In what follows in this book, you'll see fewer Bible references than you might expect. Certainly, God used specific chapters and verses to shape my life. But more than that, he reoriented my worldview to understand what happened to my family, where He was when it happened, and what I'm supposed to think and do about it. Don't be misled, I needed to be comforted and corrected, and the Bible was the sufficient source-book for His work in me. It must be the textbook for all gospel ministry to the wounded. His word is true, trustworthy, and sufficient for this work.

Part II.
Immediate Care

3.
Talk to the Healer

I was 'd- d- down with the DC Talk'.[1] Sure, I was well-versed in a variety of church music. I could hold my own at a hymn-sing, even memorizing the hymn number for the most popular songs. Southern Gospel was no problem either. I even sported the feathered-back, heavily-sprayed hairdo for a brief period. And I could join in with the mainstream CCM (Contemporary Christian Music) artists. To this day, I'm pretty sure I can sing every word of Michael W.

---

1. From DC Talk, 'Luv is a verb', https://www.youtube.com/watch?v=WRfFuhrdGKM – accessed on 3/22/2017.

Smith's 'Friends'. Despite being rhythmically-challenged, though, Christian rap was my top game. On more than one youth trip, I rode in the back seat on the church bus and threw down some from DC Talk. Better believe I was *Free at Last*.[2]

Few will forget the hip-hop artist who straddled the line between secular and contemporary Christian music during that period, Stanley Kirk Burrell. We knew him simply as M.C. Hammer. Who can forget his Hammer pants and most popular song, 'U Can't Touch This'? It's one of his other songs that I sing with some frequency even today. Thankfully, I almost always sing it in my head (complete with the high-pitched background part, too) and not out loud, but the lyrics live on nonetheless. The title of the song is simply, 'Pray'.

The lyrics aren't masterful and the theology is a little wonky, but the rhythm is catchy and the words are memorable. And the main word is one I need to hear, every single day: *pray*.

The twelve-year-old me had plenty of needs, and no one near me was capable of meeting all of them: not my parents nor youth minister nor Sunday school teacher. None of them could heal the wounds caused by the trauma I had experienced. Only One can heal.

Now you and I fully know that we're supposed to pray. We don't need M.C. Hammer or this little book to tell us to pray. Or do we? Think back to recent crises in your church family. I have no doubt that you prayed with each person and family. Certainly you shared the request

---

2. Title of a DC Talk Album.

appropriately and led your church leadership to pray. Perhaps you even faithfully remembered them in your private prayer time. If so, then allow me to pile on some encouragement as I suspect few of us pray with the zeal and consistency that we want. Thus, allow me to restate the obvious. When a person you know is suffering from the result of someone else's sin, they need you to intercede regularly, zealously, and specifically for them. They need a friend like the persistent widow in the parable who will cry out to the Lord day and night on their behalf.

I'm confident that every evangelical pastor who reads this book will affirm the importance of prayer in these situations. Yet often our response to a crisis places prayer near the end of a long list of actions. We call, visit, confront, advise, cook meals, babysit kids; we do a myriad of useful tasks. But we forget to pray. Instead of trying to re-convince the convinced, I'd like to share some wisdom on prayer and tease out the implications for ministry to those in crisis.

I've been helped immensely by an article I read several years ago by David Powlison on prayer.[3] Primarily, he addresses pastoral prayer in the church's public gatherings that focus too much on temporal needs like physical sickness. He argues that in these situations it can become 'either a dreary litany of familiar words, or a magical superstition verging on hysteria'. In truth, we don't need him to tell us about it.

When it comes to ministry to those who are suffering like I was, his counsel is very important. As our family

---

3. David Powlison, 'Praying Beyond the Sick List'. *The Journal of Biblical Counseling*, Volume 23, Number 1 (Winter 2005), pp. 2-6.

dissolved, we had a wide variety of needs: such as a place to live, immediate financial support, and a job for both of my parents. I'm grateful that people prayed for these needs and many were actually instruments in meeting them. But we mustn't stop here.

Powlison contends that when you examine the prayers in the Bible, you find three distinct and inter-related emphases.

First, *sometimes the prayers are asking God to change the circumstances.* Whether we're asking God to heal a sickness, provide for daily needs, protect us from suffering, convert unbelieving friends and family, provide a spouse, quiet a dangerous storm, end a drought, or give us a child, these circumstantial prayers are good and right. This type of prayer is often our default and is a valuable instrument of grace in the midst of a crisis. Don't forget that people in crisis have immediate and ongoing needs. They need food, shelter, clothing, and similar, and God is the provider of all good things. So don't forget to bring these requests to Him.

Second, *sometimes we pray wisdom prayers.* In these times we are asking God to change us and not our circum-stances. Here we ask God to deepen our faith, teach us to love each other, forgive our sins, give us wisdom, help us to know Him better, sanctify us, give us freedom from sin, help us understand Scripture, or teach us how to encourage others.

My aim is not to provide a full theology of suffering, but wisdom prayers are necessary in crisis because God allows these moments and uses them to shape His people. I was careful to avoid the word 'accident' in the Introduction because what happened to my family was not the result of misfortune. The only wise God put me in this family and He was not surprised by the events of the summer of '89. To borrow loosely from Joseph in Genesis 45, God sent me there for His purposes.

With more than twenty-five years of separation I can see the gracious hand of God's providence, but those hurting are not ready to hear it when the wounds are still fresh. So until it's time to talk to them about it (and that's coming later), talk to God about it. Again, think of Joseph. From the time his brothers sell him into slavery until the day they meet again in Egypt, likely two decades have passed. Joseph went from the pit to prison to the palace and he's been serving in a high position of leadership for nine years. We're not told much about his journey to forgiveness or his insight into God's purposes along the way. But we can be certain that his perspective reflects wisdom and discernment. He needed it, and so did I.

When walking beside someone after a crisis, pray wisdom prayers for them. At times we will be able to see the situation objectively and have perspective they don't. But rather than attempting to explain it, pray for God to illumine their hearts to see it.

Third, *sometimes we pray kingdom prayers*. Through these prayers, 'we ask God to change everything by revealing Himself more fully on the stage of real life, magnifying the degree to which His glory and rule are obvious'.[4] The clouds of discouragement and despair descend upon us when we face trials, but the light of the glory of God is not diminished. Our view of our circumstances might be

---

4. ibid., p. 4.

obstructed, but He is still good and kind and mighty. Pray that, even while the circumstances are dark, He will shine the light of hope in an unmistakable way.

I don't know of anyone in my situation who knew about Powlison's three strands of prayer, or if he had written about it before 1989. I have no evidence of people who prayed this way for me. But this pattern emerges from Jesus' teaching in the Sermon on the Mount – and God answered all three of these prayers in my life.

Matthew 6:9-13 is commonly called the Lord's prayer. Notice how each strand emerges in Jesus' sample prayer.

> Our Father in heaven,
> hallowed be your name.
> Your kingdom come,
> your will be done,
> on earth as it is in heaven.
> Give us this day our daily bread,
> and forgive us our debts,
> as we also have forgiven our debtors.
> And lead us not into temptation,
> but deliver us from evil.

He begins with kingdom prayer, inviting God to rule here the way He does in heaven. Then He asks God to meet physical, practical needs. Finally, He asks God to protect and shape our hearts and minds. Again, we shouldn't try to press this pattern rigidly over every prayer, or make it an absolute rule. But notice the balance it brings to our intercession.

As I reflect, God answered *circumstantial prayers* for us. My mom found a steady job that provided for our basic needs. We found a place to live and I can never recall a time of going without food and shelter. At times, God's provision was very ordinary. My mom earned a paycheck and she paid bills, or my dad sent money and we used it to buy groceries. Other times, God's provision was extraordinary. Someone met a need when we didn't expect it or generously provided when we didn't have means. God gave us our daily bread.

More importantly, God answered *wisdom prayers*. I'm still in the process of healing and learning from the trauma of my experience. But God has been so gracious to shape my perspective. I can say with Joseph, 'God sent me here for his purposes.' And let that be a guide for us as we pray:

> God, will you work in the heart of those who are hurting, so that they can see your gracious hand in their situation and come to glorify you? Let them see that your sovereignty didn't diminish when tragedy struck; you were not off your throne or asleep. Instead, will you, over the course of the next months and years, bring them to the point of knowing that even this disaster will resound for your glory and their good? God, give them wisdom to see with your eyes and glorify you.

Finally, God answered *kingdom prayers*. I hope in writing this book to direct your attention to the light of the glory of God. His kingdom has not yet been fully realized in my life. He continues to convict me of sin and transform my life, but through my crisis He is displaying His worth. Why would a pastor's kid walk through what I did and grow up to love Christ and pursue pastoral ministry? Because God is able to change everything on the stage of real life to magnify His worth in the world.

God, will you so move in our churches that the people who are most wounded by sin are among the very ones you so powerfully transform? May your glory in the gospel shine a light into the darkness of this world through the unmistakable life-transformation of the people we expected to wilt or walk away. May you raise up men and women for your purposes who at one time were cast aside and downtrodden under the weight of someone else's sin. God, change everything so your kingdom becomes more visible.

I'll never know how many people prayed for me or how often they lifted up my family, but God heard their prayers. I have a dear friend, Regina, who today lives on the other side of the world, serving as a career missionary in a closed country. Twenty-five years ago, when my world was collapsing, she was my mom's closest friend. I could make a list of the tangible ways she served our family over the years, but I am confident her greatest contribution to my life was prayer. I know she prayed for me then, and that she still does. Only God knows the difference her prayers have made.

As you approach people in crisis who are suffering because of another person's sin, you may be tempted to speak or act. Before you say a word to them, offer counsel, or direct a person to a scriptural truth, pray. Pray bold, sweeping, specific prayers for their circumstances and their soul. And don't stop. By all means, do the other stuff, but don't stop praying because you've 'got to pray/ Just to make today'.[5]

---

5. From M.C. Hammer, 'Pray'.

4.
Thorough Examination

On 20 May 2013 a tornado struck Moore, Oklahoma, killing twenty-four people, injuring more than two hundred, and leaving a fourteen-mile swath of destruction. I'll never forget watching the NBC Nightly News in the days that followed and hearing news reporters applaud the quick response and hard work of Southern Baptist Disaster Relief volunteers. NBC News reporter Harry Smith said, 'If you're waiting for the government, you're gonna be in for an awful long wait. The Baptist men, they're gonna get it done tomorrow.'

I enjoyed those Matthew 5:16 moments as the secular news media drew attention to the yellow-shirt-wearing men and women who show up every time a large-scale disaster strikes. As a Southern Baptist, I'm certainly proud of the tireless effort and coordination of our denomination in responding to crises all around the world. But I'm not surprised. Every church family I've been a part of has known how to do disaster relief. I can't recall any formal training days, but they've all known what to do.

A few months after my parents' divorce, my maternal grandmother died suddenly and tragically. By the time my mom, brother, and I, made it home, the first responders were in full swing. Food came in by the truck-loads that day and all manner of crying and hugging continued through the evening. Not many of those folks knew my grandmother, but they knew us. They didn't come in yellow shirts, but they were doing disaster relief. While I didn't fully appreciate it as a kid, it was a beautiful picture of the church in action.

Some crises, like deaths, are easier for these first responders. They've been down that road before and there are clear and appropriate responses. Nobody wants to think about cooking in those moments so food always hits the spot. A quick visit, with appropriate questions about the deceased, expressions of concern and love, and a prayer, is helpful and encouraging. When our family careened into the ditch, I'm grateful that we had a church full of first responders who knew how to respond when my grandmother died.

But some crises, like divorce or drug overdose, that doesn't end in death or criminal charges, are not as easy for these first responders. The lines of appropriateness aren't as clear. The questions aren't as obvious. The expressions of concern and love aren't as apparent. I'm not blaming them or condemning them. None of us knows quite what to do or say.

Our family's implosion affected me personally and it rocked our congregation. Opinions and questions abounded. Some people struggled to know what to say and I can appreciate the awkwardness of the situation because everything had changed. Some people fished for information on my parents and our ongoing situation. It's natural to want to know; curiosity is normal. At times the right question is the best instrument to begin a meaningful conversation. But the line between excessive inquisitiveness and genuine concern gets blurry.

When a natural disaster or physical crisis occurs, a bevy of activity follows. Lights flash and sirens blare. Police officers secure the scene. Emergency medical technicians and paramedics triage and treat the injured. Fire personnel assist in numerous ways. Again, that's our frame of reference.

One of the best instruments of grace in those moments of immediate care is silence. I'm a words guy. I talk, preach sermons and teach Bible studies. I counsel people, and make hospital visits, home visits, and phone calls. As the dust settles from the crisis, there will be lots of words. But, pastors, we mustn't fail to pray and then listen.

I admit to not loving awkward silence. When it's too quiet I'm prone to speak, or even to hum. In fact, if there is too much silence over a meal, I'll make a 'mmmmm' sound as I'm taking a bite. Even if I don't like the food, the noise comes rolling out because it's an involuntary response to silence; I'm not made for it. But in response to crisis, silence is a powerful instrument of God's grace.

Even more, our silence allows us to listen, which is a vital aspect of immediate care.

To paint with broad strokes, there seem to be two types of people in crisis: talkers and non-talkers.

If you visit a family at a funeral home after the sudden loss of a loved one, you'll see what I mean. Inevitably, there's someone – a daughter or son, a parent or grandparent, an aunt or uncle – who takes charge of the moment. When I'm going to preach at or lead the funeral service, these folks are invaluable. He or she will be ready to talk. He will ask the questions that need to be asked; she will communicate the information that I need to know. Always ready to speak for the family and to help in obvious and tangible ways, these people seem to be spurred on to action by the pain of the moment.

Then there are the quiet ones. Crippled under the weight of grief, or shaken by the suddenness of it all, they don't know what to say. They don't want to answer questions and they're more than willing to defer.

Neither reaction is better or worse, but they are very different and almost always present. I'm convinced that while personality may drive the way a person responds, past experiences are a primary factor in determining a person's response. Again, both are appropriate reactions to tragic loss, and most of us default to one or the other. I mention it not to attack or defend anyone. Instead, I want to reinforce the challenge of listening well.

Let's start with the quiet ones. This group seems more difficult, especially to me. While most of my job requires talking, I'm naturally introverted. So when I have prepared comments, I'm good to go, but small talk situations wear me out. Enter the non-talker. This presents more of an immediate challenge to me personally, but it doesn't affect ministering to them as much as you might think. These folks don't say much, but every sentence is full. They may not express things eloquently, but every word seems to convey the raw, heart-level truth about how they're feeling. Again, the challenge is getting them to say anything.

Not so much with the talkers. You'd think it would be easier to listen to them, and on one level it certainly is. You don't have to prod them along or ask insightful questions. Simply stand or sit nearby, look them in the eyes, and nod interestingly. I'm really not making fun at all; it's just easier to hear from the talkers. They're doing fine, but they're worried about so-and-so. He's bottling it all up inside and hasn't said much. They can think clearly and can even perform the eulogy at the funeral if needed. Don't misunderstand, they're not emotionally cold or distant; they just don't seem overwhelmed or even shaken. But listening to them is more difficult because they don't usually say anything substantive about themselves. They talk, but you have to listen with a discerning ear to catch what's going on spiritually.

Again, I describe these two types of people in broad strokes not to play to stereotypes or insult anyone. I was in a crisis at twelve years of age, and I wasn't much of a talk-about-your-feelings kind of kid. I'm sure my parents – and judging by my conduct grades in elementary school, my teachers too – would attest to the fact that I talked more than was necessary. But I didn't want to talk about what was going on in my home or in my head. The truth is, I couldn't even make sense of it. In many ways, God is still shaping my heart and mind. The exercise of writing this book has been more helpful to me than I ever dreamed as I continue to see God's hand in it. Anyway, as a teenager I didn't understand and couldn't express what I was feeling or thinking. But I'm grateful because God sent men and women who listened carefully to me along the way.

As you probably know, the biblical book of Job tells the story of a guy who lost pretty much everything: his home, his kids, his health, and almost his sanity. The bulk of the book, however, tells about the conversations he had with his friends. His friends aren't exactly heroes in the story as their perspective and advice is not all that helpful or godly. But at the beginning of the story they do something really well. They sit with Job and commiserate.

> And when they saw him from a distance, they did not recognize him. And they raised their voices and wept, and they tore their robes and sprinkled dust on their heads toward heaven. And they sat with him on the ground seven days and seven nights, and no one spoke a word to him, for they saw that his suffering was very great. (Job 2:12-13)

Just be there.

For several reasons, I try to avoid names in telling my story: first, the individual is not as important as the God who used them; second, some people don't want to be named; and third, there's no way to mention everyone, so I fear hurting some by their exclusion. But my story can't be understood without realizing the impact of two people: my youth minister and his wife. Duane was a high school science teacher, football coach, deacon in our church, and eventually volunteer youth minister. He and his wife Teri are two of the most significant instruments of grace in my story. They didn't formally adopt me because I didn't need to be adopted. I had parents who, even though broken, were still present and very much interested in parenting me. I never shared their address, although I did claim a portion of a closet for several years. The list of everything they've done for me over the years would roll on for hours. They met physical, emotional, and spiritual needs. But as much as anything, they listened.

Folks who know Duane are going to laugh that I mention him in a chapter about listening. I doubt anyone would list that as one of his primary strengths, but I would. He is a classic people-person. He's the life of every party he's ever attended, and somehow even the life of parties he didn't attend. His personality is immediately magnetic and he's always having fun. Nearly everyone loves him right away and secretly hopes he'll be their new best friend. I could go on listing clichés but I think you get the idea. He's the talker, so the seven days of silence from Job chapter 2 never happened.

To this day, I don't think he had a sophisticated strategy, but he came and sat with me. He didn't tear his clothes or sprinkle dust on his head, but he shed some tears along the way. Actually, on second thought, he didn't come and sit with me. He came and picked me up and made me work. He was always busy: busy working or thinking or talking, or all three at the same time. He didn't want to sit inside all day reading books and drinking coffee. Not that there's anything wrong with that. He just wanted to be on the move. There was always firewood to chop, stack, or restack. I promise there was one day we took wood off the stack just to restack in the same place more efficiently. There was always a car to wash, a piano to move, a house to paint, or a deck to build. Those aren't hypothetical examples, as I can tell you the specific stories.

For the better part of five years, whatever he was doing I was expected to do with him. And he didn't want me because I was particularly useful. I advanced rather slowly at learning to drive a nail or chop firewood. But I wasn't there for him as much as I was there for me. I'm sure I slowed down his work, bending nails in the deck and leaving dirty spots on his truck as I washed it. The Lord only knows the thousands of dollars I consumed in groceries, and the family time I interrupted. I'm certain I was a mild inconvenience at times and an outright headache at others. But there he was, week after week, working, talking, and listening.

Teri was there, too, but in a different way. She was warm and kind, and she was much quieter. For obvious reasons, I didn't spend the same amount of time with her, but she played a similar and vital role nonetheless: always listening and encouraging, usually offering to make me a sandwich. Did I mention, she was always listening?

Their hearts broke for me and my situation. Duane and Teri couldn't fix it, but they could sit with me and commiserate. Again, it didn't look like sack-cloth, ashes, and silence, but they were listening nonetheless. They welcomed me in, invited me along, and listened. They grew to know me very well, saw through my self-righteousness more than once, and called me to surrender fully to Christ. But I'm getting ahead of myself.

In the midst of crisis, no matter the personality type, it takes time to hear the heart of the hurting person. This type of listening won't happen only during 'counseling sessions' or formal Bible studies. Often they don't know what to say or how to say it, but the truth will leak out slowly. It did with me. Fortunately, God sent men and women who were listening after the cyclone of sin devastated my heart.

Part III.
Intensive Care

5.
Diagnose the Heart

Scripture passages like 1 Timothy 3 and Titus 1 explain that men who serve in the pastoral role ought to live exemplary lives. The qualifications are not, in and of themselves, extraordinary. Yet the church must only affirm men in this role who exhibit these ordinary characteristics extraordinarily. While no man lives up to the standard perfectly, by God's grace pastors should garner respect from believers and unbelievers based on their lives. Hopefully, there are aspects of the pastor's life – particularly his heart for holiness and the exercise of his gifts – that are impressive displays of the Spirit's power. So while no one should be enamored by their pastor, pastors had better be pacing the congregation 'in speech, in conduct, in love, in faith, [and] in purity' (1 Tim. 4:12).

With that in mind, every pastor needs a small group of people who are thoroughly unimpressed by him. He needs a group of people living closely enough to him to see the quality and normalcy of his life. They will see that by God's grace he meets the qualifications for elder leadership, but will at times laugh with him – and at him even before he knows what he's done that was so funny! They will love and learn from his biblical knowledge and gifting, but won't stand in awe of him. They will appreciate the Lord's work the way God is using him, but realize he's a goof-ball most of the time.

For many reasons I'm so grateful to my wife. We started dating in high school and have been dating, engaged, or married for more than half our lives. I can say with confidence that she is thoroughly unimpressed with me. She knows the truth; she knows that sometimes I have to ask my ten-year-old, spelling-bee-champion daughter how to spell words. She still has the cassette tape of my first sermon. I will assure you that it's the most excruciating eight minutes of audio ever recorded, but she can verify it. There's not enough money in the world to make me play that tape, but she could be coaxed into sharing it. Do you know why? She's already unimpressed with me. I think she's thoroughly impressed with God and what He is able to do, and appreciates the grace of God in getting me this far. But she's not asking for my autograph.

While I wouldn't have said it twenty years ago, I'm very grateful she's not impressed. I don't need her to be the head of my fan club. The truth is, I don't deserve a fan club at all, but you get what I'm saying. When I'm an idiot, I need her to speak candidly to me. Unfortunately, I provide her with frequent opportunities to fulfil this role. And fortunately, she's willing to follow through candidly. She's not the only one, either. I need godly men who know me well enough to see through my self-righteousness and confront my sin.

This instrument of grace – the loving confrontation of sin – is not merely for pastors. The ministry to people in crisis that I've described up to this point has been fairly easy. Love people, pray for them, and listen to them. It's not without sacrifice, but it's fairly easy. In the wake of the immediate crisis, that's perfect.

There comes a moment, though, when the wounded person needs to be lovingly confronted with truth. As I mentioned before, my goal is not to provide a theology of suffering, but it bears repeating that suffering is an instrument of grace. God allows us to suffer as a result of other people's sin so that He can continue His work in us. He is at work to conform Christians into the image of His Son, and everything occurs by His providence and for our good. Romans 8:28-30 is true:

> And we know that for those who love God all things work together for good, for those who are called according to his purpose. For those whom he foreknew he also predestined to be conformed to the image of his Son, in order that he might be the firstborn among many brothers. And those whom he predestined he also called, and those whom he called he also justified, and those whom he justified he also glorified.

63

God is not just making a big cup of divine lemonade out of the nasty bag of lemons. He's not reacting to our suffering with a back-up plan to get us back on track: suffering is part of the track. As the healing begins, someone must say this to the sufferer. Even more, you must confront at least one sin in the wounded person's heart: pride.

As I reflect back on those years, two sins grew in my heart following the trauma. Both stem from a singular root: pride. Remember, I was the clip-on-tie-wearing, Bible-drill king. I could play the game and look the part. I knew the difference between Barnabas and Barabbas, and that the guy who sentenced Jesus to execution was Pilate and not pilot. I'm not trying to brag or boast; I'm trying to paint the picture for you.

In Philippians 3, Paul confronts pride in the false teachers by listing his accomplishments and then comparing them to dung. He reminds them that he satisfied the outward requirements of the law, but says anything that might be considered gain is now loss when compared with knowing Christ. While I don't remember ever saying it this way, I liked about half of Paul's paragraph.

I could track with the first part. Here was my version of verses 4-6! If anyone else thinks he has reason for confidence in the flesh, I have more: *baptized* in the *sixth* year, of the *pastor's family*, of the tribe of *Southern Baptists*, a *Baptist* of *Baptists*; as to the law, a *Pharisaical little boy*; as to zeal, a *condescending judge* of the more *glaring sinners*; as to righteousness under the law, blameless in *my own mind*. Full stop.

I'm not proud of it, but that's who I was. The bigger problem, however, was that I didn't see it. I needed people to tell me. I recall meditating on this passage as a high school student and finally seeing the second half of that paragraph. With a little help from Michael English's version of the song 'In Christ Alone', the words came to life.

> But whatever gain I had, I counted as loss for the sake of Christ. Indeed, *I count everything as loss because of the surpassing worth of knowing Christ Jesus my Lord.* For his sake I have suffered the loss of all things and count them as rubbish, in order that I may gain Christ and be found in him, not having a righteousness of my own that comes from the law, but that which comes through faith in Christ, the righteousness from God that depends on faith – that I may know him and the power of his resurrection, and may share his sufferings, becoming like him in his death, that by any means possible I may attain the resurrection from the dead. (Phil. 3:7-11, emphasis mine)

I was a broken mess and pride was manifesting itself in two primary ways: self-pity and self-righteousness.

Self-pity is an ugly version of pride that produces a sympathy symphony – and I was prone to play this tune. Think back with me. I was the poor, twelve-year-old victim of an awful situation. Despite my charming wit, winning personality, and exuding Christ-likeness, my family imploded. I mean, I didn't deserve this. I didn't always strike the chords of self-pity on purpose, but I did nothing to stop the music. Poor me. As much as I allowed others to say it, I said it to myself. Not out loud, but in the quiet places I lamented the consequences of my life. I secretly despised the inconveniences of a single-parent lifestyle, weekend visitations, and a complicated family dynamic. More than merely playing on others' sympathy, I harbored bitterness and resentment at my parents and at God for my situation.

Then came self-pity's ugly cousin, self-righteousness. Pride in this form makes comparisons with others to make you feel better. Again, I didn't deserve this. I knew better than to voice the sentiment, but surely others warranted a familial implosion more than I did. They weren't as faithful to church activities. They didn't know Jacob and Israel were two names for the same guy. They didn't know Hezekiah was a king and not a book of minor prophecy in the Old Testament. They couldn't even say the books of the New Testament in order. I created a view of myself compared to others that made my heart ripe for this sin. Not only could I play the religious game, but everyone was telling me how great I was at it. I was more than happy to agree with them.

The longer I serve in pastoral ministry the more convinced I become that victims of someone else's sin default to self-pity and self-righteousness. The spouse betrayed by adultery. The parent grieving over a rebellious child. The victim of sexual abuse. The family mourning death at the hands of a drunk driver. When our parents, child, co-worker, or a drunk driver sins and brings immediate harm upon us, pride is crouching at the door. It's there all along, but suffering gives it a moment of opportunity.

Know that I sit in the seat of confession and not condemnation. I needed (and I still need) the gospel. I needed the gospel to remind me that *I* was a sinner. Yes, everyone else was a sinner and because of some of their specific sins, my life was a mess. I played that recording over and over. I could play it at home, at church, at school. In fact, I could go all the way back to the Garden of Eden and play the self-pitying, self-righteous blame-game with Adam and Eve in Genesis 3. They ate the fruit and ruined the whole thing. Thanks a lot. But the gospel destroyed that recording and reminded me that while I didn't eat the actual piece of fruit in the garden, I had eaten the fruit thousands of times.

The gospel reminded me that my parents were culpable for some of my hurt, but I was no better than they were. The gospel made it abundantly clear that I didn't deserve the trauma I was experiencing; I deserved much worse. I deserved the wrath of God for my sin. Until confronted with my depravity, I took a seat up on a throne. But thanks be to God for exposing my sin.

Enter two other formative influences in my life in the form of another young couple in our church, Tommy and Dawn. They served in lots of roles over the years that I can remember. He was a deacon, sang in the choir, and led short-term mission trips. She taught Sunday school, played in nearly every support role you can name, and wrote some fantastic skits for our youth gathering. During my middle-school years, I saw them almost every day because I rode the school bus to their house. Over the years I stayed at their house more nights than I can count.

It's impossible to crystallize almost a decade of direct influence into one paragraph, but I mention them here because of one story that illustrates a part of their role in my life. To this day, I say 'no thank you' instead of 'nope' because of this couple. Dawn was quick-witted, but always accommodating. Tommy was hospitable, but blunt. He would do anything in the world to help you, but if you presumed grace he'd call you out for it. As I recall, it was a fairly normal afternoon when I responded rather abruptly in declining something Dawn had offered me. He interjected in a way I would never forget. It was one of the most undramatic, but significant events of my life. He didn't physically threaten or berate me verbally. I didn't recoil in fear or end up in the fetal position. He firmly, but lovingly reminded me of how to speak kindly and respectfully to a lady.

Tommy obviously cared for me and ached for the trauma I experienced, but he wasn't going to overlook disrespect in even the simplest form. I didn't see a ray of light from heaven that day or agonize in confession before God that night. The event seems much more significant today than it did then. It acts as more of an illustration than a spiritual marker. God used the steady influence of this couple and others like them to show me the reality of my sinfulness more clearly.

Let me clarify. I've been in the process of healing for more than two decades and I'm not pretending that I was ready for these truths right away. Often the victims of sin are never pressed to realize that they are contributing members of the sinful condition of our world. Even sufferers need people to speak candidly but cautiously about the situation and how to move forward. The path to forgiveness and healing in my family went straight through the wilderness of my own sin. I was the chief of sinners in my home and my failure to understand and appreciate that separated me from the power of the gospel to free me from hurt, anger, bitterness, and resentment.

But by God's providence, I was in the wreckage for His glory and *my* good. Our family careened off the road so that God would crush sin in *me*. But that's not what I thought in 1989 and that's not what I wanted to hear. Thankfully, I was still a kid and under the authority and care of adults. They were thoroughly unimpressed with me and willing to confront my sin. Because they did, the gospel was not just the answer for my dad; it was the power of God to save me.

Let's go back to Joseph in Genesis 37–50. When his brothers show up in Egypt, they meet a different man. Physically, they don't recognize him, but the inward change is more dramatic. The cool-coat-wearing, crazy-dreamer kid is now a man. He walked a hard road of suffering: from slavery to false accusations, to unjust imprisonment to being forgotten. The man who refuses to seek revenge against his brothers must have been shaped by the transforming grace of God. Hebrews 11 hints at what held him firm: 'By faith Joseph ...'

At some point along the way – likely long before the brothers arrive in Egypt – Joseph forgives. While his path of repentance toward God and reconciliation with Him by faith is not spelled out, we know it took place. For the thread of the Bible and his inclusion in Hebrews 11 confirms it to us.

When a person is confronted by his own sin and drawn to repent, the gospel shapes his perspective of others. The gospel knocks us down from the throne we've created and assumed for ourselves, forcing us to acknowledge and admit that we're all the same. Their sin and my sin are equally offensive to God's holiness. Here's where steady investment in those who are hurting over the long term makes a critical difference. When the other person's sin seems big and the consequences far-reaching, it can envelop our sin in an ominous black cloud, at least from our perspective. The fire and smoke of the other's disastrous, family-shattering sin creates a haze that blinds us from seeing our self-pity and self-righteousness. If we're going to minister well, though, we must shine the light of the gospel through the dark clouds.

I hope pastor-shepherds and Christian leaders will understand that faithful, loving care for the wounded in a crisis will create a platform for the confrontation of sin later on. None is righteous, no not one. We must never forget that suffering is an instrument of grace to sanctify us. Victims tend to forget that sanctification is ongoing as they plead with God to work immediately in their offenders' lives. As victims, we cry out, 'God, fix them so it won't hurt anymore' and, 'God, break them and lead them to repentance so reconciliation can occur'.

Comparison however is a great enemy of repentance. Hold up the mirror of Christ's life and make the person see the reality of her sin. For only then will God use the gospel to do His work in her. My parents' divorce wasn't my sin, but I had plenty of my own. I was still responsible to honor God; I needed to trust Him, and not myself. I needed to run to Him and His word, not good works and achievement. I needed to remember God's grace to forgive me and in turn to forgive my parents.

6.
Daily Treatment

In trying to teach my young son to play basketball there are many aspects of the game he must understand. First, there are rules. He can't run with the ball without dribbling, or take the ball outside the boundaries, or hit another player. A basket counts as two points, unless it's a free throw or is shot from behind a particular line.

Second, there are techniques for individual success. He should be able to dribble with either hand. He should shoot primarily with one hand while balancing the ball with the other, and should learn how to shoot from the top of his jump. He should fight for position when someone else shoots the ball, and rebound with two hands.

Third, there are techniques for team success. He needs to learn to pass the ball, and how to position himself on the court to help other team members. He needs to learn to play with a selfless attitude that will foster team success.

While a lack of knowledge in these areas can prevent him from developing into a good basketball player, understanding these things will not necessarily make him a good player, either. The basketball world is full of coaches, analysts, and fans who understand the basic (and even the complex) aspects of the game, but have little or no ability to play the game physically. To know about the game is only one step in excelling at it.

Similarly, I was as much of a twelve-year-old Bible expert as I've ever known. While in the grand scheme I knew very little, compared to other kids my age I was well-advanced. Even more, I didn't really understand how the gospel was supposed to shape me. A lack of knowledge of the gospel prevents life transformation, but as G.I. Joe taught me, knowing these things was only half the battle. My greatest need was to embrace the transformation God brings through the gospel.

The gospel will never shape a life unless it first invades the head. God does not bypass the brain; He goes through it. Noted author and Christian apologist J. P. Moreland contends that 'the key to change is the formation of a new perspective, the development of fresh insights about our lives and the world around us, the gathering of the knowledge and skill required to know what to do and how to do it.'[1] While Moreland's comment deserves more explanation and qualification than I am able to offer here, clearly he is striking an important note. In the context of his book, he's speaking broadly to spiritual maturity. He continues, 'The mind ... plays a fundamental role in the process of human maturation and change, including spiritual transformation.'[2]

We must be careful to qualify that knowledge is not an end, but a means. Many men and women have fully understood the meaning of the words and phrases in the Bible, and been able to recall passages and stories from memory, while never experiencing life-transformation. As we move on to the second aspect of intensive care, in this process of helping someone heal from the trauma of another person's sin, we come finally to teaching. Having addressed the more general aspects of this ministry – namely, that the gospel is ground for our approach and the Bible is our undergirding sourcebook – we turn now to specific instruction in godliness.

Sin disrupts life and it distorts a person's view of herself. It shatters our world and can even shake our faith. It's critical that someone reminds sufferers that our identities in Christ do not change even when everything in our world collapses. Let this chapter encourage us to remind sufferers of who we are in Christ.

It's well documented that the apostle Paul followed a simple but definite pattern in his more systematic and

---

1. J. P. Moreland, *Love the Lord Your God with All Your Mind: The Role of Reason in the Life of the Soul* (Colorado Springs, CO: Nav Press, 2012), p. 66.

2. ibid., p. 67.

theological letters in the New Testament. All thirteen of the letters attributed to him in the Bible are occasional, meaning that he wrote to a specific group of people at a specific time for a specific reason. While every letter presents important theological material, two of them present concepts in a more systematic and thorough manner. In contrast to Philippians, which reads like a thank you note, or Titus, which gives instructions for a young pastor, Romans and Ephesians provide a more complete explanation of the gospel and the implications for all of life.

Back to the pattern, scholars and even casual readers observe a specific shift in both of these letters from the indicative mood to the imperative mood. The indicative mood is a verb form whereby the author makes a declarative statement: 'The dog is dirty.' In contrast, the imperative mood is a verb form whereby the author makes a command or request of the reader: 'Give the dog a bath.'

Theologically and practically, the movement from indicative to imperative is a very important concept to understand and apply. At the risk of oversimplification, the first eleven chapters of Romans make theologically-indicative statements. God reveals Himself to humans. Humans reject God and rebel against Him: they neither acknowledge Him as God nor worship Him. Humans also mistreat one another. As a result of this sin, we face the wrath of God. God's Son, Jesus, died as a propitiation for our sin. All who believe in Jesus for salvation will escape God's wrath and have eternal life. Beginning in chapter 12, Paul shifts gears dramatically and begins riddling readers with a barrage of imperative statements. Use your spiritual gifts faithfully. Hate what is evil and cling to what is good.

Don't be lazy in your zeal. Pray constantly. Show hospitality. I could keep going, but I think you get the point.

Paul follows the same pattern in Ephesians. The first three chapters are indicative. We were dead. God made us alive, for by grace we have been saved. The last three chapters are imperative. Walk worthy of your calling. Bear with one another in love. Speak truth with your neighbour. The apostle tells them who they are before he tells them what to do. Got it?

This pattern is neither accidental nor incidental. Paul did not stumble upon this approach. It wasn't just a literary device, and it isn't a minor point. It's more than a neat fact about these letters to include in a seminary exam. Understanding the pattern helps to unlock the power of the gospel to shape and transform us.

Having explained the basic gospel message in chapters 1–4 of Romans (briefly addressed within chapter 1), Paul addresses the effects of this salvation in the life of the believer in chapters 5–8. On the foundation of this basic message of man's need and God's provision, he explains that this salvation transforms us by uniting us with Christ and freeing us from sin and its power. He describes this transformation in chapter 6. In commenting on this description, John Stott notes eight declarations he makes about believers.[3] These statements show how the gospel continues transforming us after the point of initial salvation.

First, believers are dead to sin. Within the question in Romans 6:2, Paul asserts that those people who have

---

3. John R. W. Stott, *The Message of Romans* (Downers Grove, IL: InterVarsity Press, 1994), pp. 168-9.

believed in God for salvation are now dead to sin. By 'dead to sin', we understand that we are now separated from the rule and reign of sin. We are no longer dominated and ruled by sin's power.

Second, believers die to sin by uniting with Christ through baptism. Building on the first thought, Paul explains in verse 3 that the power of sin dies in us when we are united to Christ. Additionally, we are united with Him through baptism. Paul is not suggesting that water baptism saves us or that 'being dunked' changes us. Rather, baptism throughout the New Testament refers to a visible sign of invisible work of the Spirit. Here again, our union with Christ is dramatically signified, set forth, and sealed in our spiritual baptism, which is illustrated in our water baptism.

Third, believers are also united with Christ in His resurrection. Our union with Christ does not end with death to sin; it also includes resurrection to new life. Notice verse 4 contains three words that tower between Paul's statement about our death to sin and our new life: *in order that*. We are united with Him in death in order that, or so that, or for the purpose that, we are united with Him in new life! Our union with Christ brings new life.

Fourth, believers are free from slavery to sin. This freedom does not mean that we will never sin again. We will not experience a decisive break from sin in this life, but we do realize a decisive break from the bondage to sin. While our old nature was under the power of sin and unable to relate to God, the new nature is free from sin's power, having access to God through faith. What dies at our conversion is not simply the bad part of us, but all of us. We escape from the penalty and power of sin through our union with Christ. This union with Christ frees us from the bondage to sin that separated us from God.

Fifth, believers are free to live for God as Christ does. Corresponding to this freedom from sin is a freedom to live in righteousness. Previously, we were prevented from living righteously by the reign of sin in our lives, but sin has now been replaced by a new King. The old self (the pre-conversion sinner who stands under God's judgment) is gone and a new self (the post-conversion, forgiven sinner who has been raised from the dead) now lives. Life now is 'resurrection anticipated'. We can now live in light of the fact that the resurrection is imminent.

Sixth, believers must realize our new position in Christ. We have to come to mentally embrace the fact of our new position in Christ. Our old pre-conversion self has been crucified and we have been raised as a new life in Christ. So, says Stott, 'We are to recall, to ponder, to grasp, to register these truths until they are so integral to our mindset that a return to the old life is unthinkable.'[4]

Seventh, believers must present themselves as instruments of righteousness. This act of offering our bodies to God is a 'deliberate and decisive commitment' to replace the old self's devotion to sin with a surrender to God.[5] Rather than allowing our bodies to follow temptation into sin, we commit our mind and will to follow Christ. This inner commitment is possible because of the freedom we have because we have been united with Him.

---

4. ibid., p. 180.

5. ibid., p. 181.

Eighth, grace leads believers away from sin and not toward it. So in response to the question Paul poses in Romans 6:1 – 'Are we to continue in sin that grace may abound?' – he answers decisively, 'no'. Grace does not lead us to sin; instead, grace leads us to recognize our new position in Christ and surrender to God.

Notice again, these are indicative statements: namely, truths about us because we have been saved. But there is more. In Romans 8 he explains how the Holy Spirit works in believers to free us from sin and lead us to obey God. Thus, salvation transforms us by uniting us with Christ and freeing us from sin and its power. This change begins in our hearts, shifting the object of our affections from ourselves to God. As this transformation takes place, our attitudes, thoughts, desires, and actions change radically. The change brought about by our union with Christ is applied to our lives through the work of the Spirit. He works in us, giving us each a new position as one who is no longer focused on earthly things, but now is focused on heavenly things. We are now sons and daughters in God's family.

This truth does not imply that a believer reaches a point of sinless perfection on earth. Instead, while sin remains a part of our earthly existence, the Spirit dwells in us, replacing our attitude of rebellion against God with an attitude of surrender to God. As believers, we bring our lives in conformity to what we now know to be true about ourselves. We kill (or mortify) behaviorally what has already been killed legally and positionally: that is, sin. The death of the deeds of the flesh is an act of reconciling our lifestyle with our new life-direction.

We do not simply embark on this sin-killing mission alone. Sin is killed 'by the Spirit'.[6] We do not achieve this by our own unaided effort, which is the error of legalism. Nor do we passively 'let go and let God' in hope that sin will go away. Here we must find the balance of actively pursuing a holiness that only comes through the power of the Spirit's work in us. We must mentally and then physically embrace the person God has now made us in Christ, by saying 'yes' to thoughts and activities that do not originate in us, but are part of our new nature.

I realize that's a fire-hydrant spray of indicative truth, but I hope you see its significance. The gospel, the story of God's plan and work to save us through Jesus, is the power of God to deliver us from the sin we never could have escaped on our own. This good news was the only message that could free me from bitterness, anger, resentment, self-pity, and self-righteousness. Before I could heal from the wounds of another, I needed to know how God had already healed me from the wounds of my own sin. I needed to know about the power of God saving me before I could lay aside the weight caused by my parents. As much as that traumatic event was shaping my view of the world, it wasn't until I stepped away from it far enough to see the light of the glory of God in the gospel, that I could see anything with clarity.

I came to heal from my wounds not by addressing them, but because the gospel changed the way I viewed myself, and then changed the way I looked at my wounds. As a twelve-year-old, I was a million miles away from these

---

6. Romans 8:13.

truths. In fact, in the process of writing this book, I'm learning more and more about how the power of God is setting me free from the power of sin in me, just as He has set me free from the wounds of others' sin.

Thus I can say this for certain: I harbor no anger or bitterness toward God or my dad for what happened when I was twelve. That fact is no testament to me; it's a testimony to the power of God in the gospel. For by grace I am being saved. Every sufferer needs a godly friend who will patiently, persistently preach the gospel first to himself and then to the one who suffers.

This is who you were. This is what God has done. This is who you now are. This is what God is doing and who He is. Now, by the power of the Holy Spirit, go be this new person.

Part IV.
Long-term Care

7.
It Takes More than Diet and Exercise

A few summers ago my wife decided we needed a vegetable garden. Despite my trepidation, we cleared a spot along the back of our house and went to work preparing the soil. With some help from a friend, we tilled the soil, added in some fertilizer, and transplanted a few plants: tomato, squash, and a small variety of peppers. We also added in some beans and potatoes.

The outcome was mixed that year. The tomato and pepper plants did just fine and we harvested all we needed for that summer. The squash plants started strong, but almost overnight they withered and died. Apparently, there's such a thing as a squash bug. Who knew? The beans and potatoes weren't a total loss, but we didn't get enough to make a single serving of a side dish. I learned plenty that summer about myself and little about gardening. More than anything, I was reminded of how grateful I was for grocery stores.

I'm not averse to work and the garden certainly demanded it: preparing, planting, watering, weeding, and harvesting. Keeping up with our little garden wasn't a full-time job, but it required more than the swipe of a debit card at the check-out aisle. I know it's obvious, but if you want to grow vegetables in a garden – even low-maintenance ones like tomatoes – the atmosphere must be right. So it is with spiritual development.

I've mentioned a few individuals who ministered to me in the wake of our family trauma and along the way. But to capture everyone who was instrumental in providing the long-term care necessary for my development, I'd need to print a list of names from an old church directory. Furthermore, this care is by God's design.

I've written plenty about the gospel – the story of God's plan and work – and how it is His power to save. God delivers us from sin's penalty, and by the continued preaching of His gospel He continues to transform us. Even more than planning and carrying out this work, God also designed the proper environment for the gospel to persist in doing its work; He established the church as the perfect setting for cultivating gospel flourishing.

Let's go back to Paul's letter to the Ephesians. After walking them through the glorious basics of the gospel in the first two chapters, he writes about his ministry in chapter 3. He was a minister of this gospel with a specific assignment to preach to Gentiles.

If you're not familiar with the biblical storyline a little background will help. Beginning in Genesis 12 with a guy named Abram (who is also more commonly called Abraham), God chooses to work primarily through a single family. He promises to make Abram's descendants into a great nation, to bless them, and to bless the whole world through them. In only a few generations this family grows rapidly and within a few hundred years they number more than 600,000 men. Soon they gain independence as a nation and are no longer thought of as merely a family. This nation was called Israel.

When Paul wrote his letters, Israel was under Roman rule and no longer had a specific geo-political empire to call its own. Nevertheless, its people held on to their ethnic and religious identity with great nationalistic pride. The Israelites, or Jews, felt spiritually superior to all the other peoples, whom they referred to as Gentiles. So it's quite controversial for Paul, a Jewish guy, to preach the gospel to Gentiles. For starters, the message originates out of the Old Testament. Jesus was a descendant from Abram and the fulfillment of all the Old Testament promises and prophecies. Secondly, the church was almost exclusively Jewish in the first couple of decades after Jesus ascended back into heaven.

Sorry for this brief history break, but hopefully now you see the potential problem with Paul preaching the gospel freely to the 'lesser' peoples. He confronts the idea in Ephesians 3 and even argues that the diversity of peoples in the church was part of God's plan all along. Note verses 8-10:

> To me, though I am the very least of all the saints, this grace was given, to preach to the Gentiles the unsearchable riches of Christ, and to bring to light for everyone what is the plan of the mystery hidden for ages in God who created all things, so that through the church the manifold wisdom of God might now be made known to the rulers and authorities in the heavenly places.

Again, Paul preaches to all kinds of peoples because it's part of God's plan. As the Creator of all peoples He uses the church, with all of her diversity, as an instrument to declare His 'manifold wisdom' in the heavenly realms. The church is the fruit of God's saving plan and a mirror to reflect His glory, or splendor and worth.

This sounds fine, but what does this have to do with twelve-year-old boys torn by divorced parents? The church – the gathering of those who trust in Christ – is the place where the gospel keeps doing its work. When the people of God gather week-to-week, they provide a God-design environment for gospel flourishing. They read and study God's word, sing about and celebrate who God is and what He has done, and illustrate and proclaim His work through baptism and the Lord's Supper. They live out gospel transformation by loving and serving one another, exhorting and encouraging one another to keep on trusting in Christ.

In the manifold wisdom of God, He created the local church to reflect His manifold wisdom. In my case it was the First Baptist Church of Belfry, Kentucky. Deep in the heart of coal country, and nestled between the foothills of the Appalachian Mountains, we met in a little brick building with a white steeple. In the midst of Sunday school classes, congregational-worship services, Wednesday prayer meetings, youth-group meetings, discipleship-training courses, men's breakfasts, Vacation Bible Schools, and choir practices, God made the gospel flourish in my soul like fast-spreading kudzu on the mountainside.

God provided fertile soil, fresh water, and sunlight. He plucked weeds and pruned branches. In thousands of un-eventful moments, He slowly and steadily shaped my heart and mind. I'm so grateful for my pastor, Steve Rice. He followed my dad as pastor and led us toward a Word-centered, gospel-shaped ministry, with a heart for the nations and a passion for individual disciple-making. I recall only a couple of his sermons specifically, but I remember him faithfully opening the Bible every week and exhorting us to understand and obey it.

There is a healthy diversity of opinion on whether or not the church should target ministry to particular groups. It can be helpful, I think, to set aside time to teach children, or youth, or men, or women. I can see the benefit of gathering those who are struggling with addiction, or grief, or parenting teenagers as well. But the person in crisis needs the church: not part of her, but the whole. In the midst of her diversity, and through the ordinariness of weekly gatherings, God keeps on tilling, planting, watering, and harvesting.

Before you get the wrong idea, though, religious activity is not the goal. Announcing and rejoicing in the glory of God is the goal – but the attendance and activity around these meetings and gatherings are not an end; they are a means. They are useful instruments employed for the purpose of glorifying God through the advancement of His gospel work. I know that's a mouthful, so let's back up a bit.

The goal of everything we do, both individually and as a church, is to glorify God. Most simply, to glorify God is to worship Him or to ascribe ultimate value and find ultimate delight in God. To paraphrase John Piper, worship is joyful satisfaction in God for who He is and what He has done, is doing, and will do that spills over into expressions of affection for God and other people.[1] Worship, then, is not essentially or primarily an outward activity although it can be seen in the outward activities it produces.

Perhaps a practical example will help. When the church gathers for weekly worship, the goal is for the people of God to worship God. Or we could say: the aim is to stimulate growth in our delight in God, and in the reflection of His worth through our lives. Most churches in North America sing, preach, pray, baptize, take the Lord's Supper, collect an offering, and make announcements. While not of equal value, each of these components can play a useful role in the weekly gathering. The aim, however, must be to shine light on God so that people will see more clearly who He is, what He has done, what He is doing, and what He will do. Thus in light of this glory, believers will be drawn to rejoice in Him so that they will love Him and others more fully.

1. John Piper, 'Gravity and Gladness on Sunday Morning' (2008). Retrieved from www.desiringgod.org/messages/gravity-and-gladness-on-sunday-morning-part-1 on 3/22/2017.

We could extend this idea to all the activities of a local church: Bible studies, choir practices, youth camp, and so on and on. My point is that for gospel growth to take hold, church members must walk alongside one another, encouraging and exhorting each other to see and delight in God. This work is not necessarily formal, and it doesn't require theological sophistication. Instead, we consistently and simply continue the work discussed in the previous chapters. We keep on speaking truth, and continue teaching identity.

Over the long term, however, there are two dangers.

First, we can get lulled to sleep thinking that, when the dust settles, the work is over. Let's move ahead a few years. As a fifteen-year-old, I attended the meetings and participated in the activities. I had pushed past the initial trauma of the crisis and adjusted to a new normal; I was doing just fine. I didn't need intensive care that continued focusing on the disaster; rather, I needed a church family.

Second, we can equate increased activity with growth in godliness. Again, the fifteen-year-old me attended the meetings and participated in the activities. Remember, I knew how to play the part. The way I viewed myself shifted slightly because I wasn't the pastor's son, but I adjusted and kept going. Once again, I had pushed past the initial trauma of the crisis and adjusted to a new normal; I was doing just fine. I didn't need intensive care that continued focusing on the disaster; rather, I needed a church.

My need was to watch real people continue to be shaped by the gospel in the context of real life: to observe people delighting in God, and reacting with increasing love for Him and for others; to notice men and women dutifully serve God through their normal vocations as school teachers, coal miners, and hospital employees; to watch men love their respective wives as Christ loves the church; to see women love their respective husbands and submit graciously to them; to watch ordinary dads and moms train up their children in the truth of God's word; and to see adults leave good jobs to follow God's call to vocational ministry.

From Denny, I needed to learn faithfulness. He always sat on the front row soaking up God's word and taking copious notes. He taught eighth grade Sunday school with his same usual zeal when only a couple of mostly-disinterested kids showed up.

From Denny's wife, Patty, I needed to learn how to sing with joy. She taught us to sing parts as a youth choir, and passionately spurred us on even though we never matched her enthusiasm for it. Then I watched this same lady bury this same man with grace and hope only a few years later. I had heard him teach about this hope, I heard her sing about this hope, and I saw her cling to it in her darkest valley. Fuelled by that hope, she still sings with the same joy even today.

From Nancy, I needed to learn hospitality and grace. She raised children without a husband in the home, and always included our family in holiday meals and cele-brations.

From Harold, I needed to learn godly conviction. I could recount numerous ways he and his wife, Susan, served faithfully in our church. Yet my most vivid memory of him comes from his courageous and gracious stand at a church business meeting. The details of the argument don't matter today, but I'll never forget his calm and confident manner that evening.

From Roger, I needed to learn how to live out the gospel at work. He was my eighth grade homeroom teacher in a public school. I watched him speak and act the same way six days a week … the same way at church and at school. With a sense of humor and seriousness for God's word, his consistency was influential.

From Joann, I needed to learn how to pray. From Peggy, I needed to learn how to use seemingly insignificant gifts to advance God's kingdom. From my pastor, Brother Steve, I needed to learn how to shepherd God's people and to preach God's word.

The list goes on and on, and on …

I needed a gospel-saturated and beautifully-unexceptional community of faith. Don't get the wrong idea; our church had her issues. My memory is of church controversies and tense business meetings. I'm certain some people stirred up dissension and others left angrily. At times the soil was too firm in places, the water too sparing, and the sunlight obstructed. Someone else will have to tell those stories, though, because that church was the garden of gospel growth in my life. For the better part of eight years, they did a variety of seemingly unremarkable things with remarkable faithfulness.

Some people seem astonished that God called me out of the ditch of my family's disaster to gospel ministry in a local church. I never have quite understood their surprise. The church was such a powerful instrument of God's grace in my life, and it's my joy to serve her. I say this not to brag or boast, but to call you to realize the necessary role of the local church in ministering to broken people. Again, we're all broken, victims of our sin and others' sin. Healing takes a long, long time, so react quickly: listen, pray, confront them with their own diagnosis. Teach them who they really are, and just keep on doing it. Don't forget that after the initial moments have passed, the work in the garden of one's heart is just getting started.

8.
Preventative Medicine

When it comes to protecting against germs, I'm a little zealous. While I'm not convinced the term germaphobe is called for, it's probably not completely inaccurate. Let's just say it this way: I try to avoid doorknobs in public, I don't drink after people (even immediate family members), and I use hand sanitizer liberally. When I fly outside the United States, it gets even worse.

Part of my international problem traces back to May 2011. That's when I participated in a mission trip to Port-au-Prince, Haiti. Not only was it my introduction to international missions, it was my first trip outside the U.S.

As I prepared for the trip, others who had gone before tried to get me ready for what I would encounter. But nothing could have prepared me for the first twenty-four hours on the ground.

Still recovering from the devastating earthquake in 2010, the conditions in Haiti were unlike anything I'd ever experienced; I was completely overwhelmed. The terminal looked like the inside of a stripped-down warehouse, the customs agent did not give the impression of legitimacy, baggage claim was mass chaos, and all manner of people were talking and yelling in a language I couldn't understand. In the years since, I've flown into a number of international airports in South America, Central America, and Africa and nothing has even come close to matching what I experienced that day.

We loaded our luggage into shopping carts and escaped the airport to a narrow, covered walkway. To the right of the walkway was the side of a building and to the left was a high chain-linked fence. While dozens of people stood opposite the fence staring at us, some men followed us along the walkway trying to help us with our bags. They spoke loudly and grabbed forcefully for our carts, hoping to help us and earn a tip. We held tightly to our luggage and walked quickly to the parking lot ahead, where our bus was waiting.

While it was my first trip to Haiti, many on our team had been on previous trips. As we made it to the dilapi-dated school bus, the reunion commenced. I couldn't have separated our welcoming committee from the airport employees, or hopeful baggage handlers, but I was swept into the fray. Hugs and handshakes multiplied all around as we threw our luggage on the bus and hurried aboard. Leaving the airport we drove through town and I saw things I never knew existed. Sixteen months after the earthquake and thousands still lived in a sprawling tent city. As we drove by, the horrifying sight of abject poverty paled in comparison to the stench of people living in crowded quarters without proper sanitation. Far worse than the toppled buildings and decimated homes was the hopelessness that filled the air.

After we arrived at our guest house and unloaded, we met for supper. My appetite was long gone, but I managed to squeeze down a few bites of spaghetti. It was mostly the same as what I'm accustomed to, but it wouldn't have mattered; I didn't feel like eating. Then one of our group leaders began our official 'orientation'. We were instructed not to drink the water: in fact, even opening your mouth in the shower, or accidently ingesting small amounts of water could be dangerous. They advised us to sanitize our hands whenever we came in contact with the water. A recent cholera outbreak set even the seasoned members of our team on high alert. I'll never forget calling my wife that night and asking, 'What have I done?' I settled down a great deal after a couple of days and the week went well. I've come to love the Haitian people and even returned in the fall of 2014.

I learned hugely about God and His global purpose on that trip; it was formative for me. In addition to the spiritual growth I experienced, my awareness of, and aversion to, germs multiplied. The best medicine against a communicable disease is good hygiene. It's not foolproof, but a dab of hand sanitizer goes a long way to reducing the risk of illness!

As my story of healing nears its end, it's important to remember that healing from sin never ends. No amount of hand sanitizer can protect us from the spiritual dangers that await. But the God who is saving us will keep on saving us.

When I was asked to consider telling this part of my story in a book, my first thought was about my dad. My goal has been to shine light on the glory of God in the gospel by sharing part of what He has done to shape my life. Following a devastating moment in my childhood, my heavenly Father was faithful. As excited as I am to tell anyone who will listen about it, the last thing I want to do is disparage my earthly father.

So in an act of godly courage, I sent him an email – seriously, I did. I'm not proud of it, but I thought it might be easier for him to read about it first. Then there was also a phone conversation at some point. Finally, we sat down for lunch. I'll never forget his one-word description of this little writing project: 'awkward'. Even though I don't understand exactly how he feels, I imagine this isn't the book he'd most want me to write.

I spoke to my mom about the book, too. Her situation is quite a bit different, but it still lays out one of the most painful parts of her life. For years, my mom has hoped and prayed that I would get the opportunity to write a book. She's a mom and that's what moms do. I can't imagine this book is what she's had in mind.

I've actually already written a book; well, a sort of book. The last step to complete a doctor of ministry degree is to complete a project and write a report. The finished product is about 125 pages or so, mostly boring seminary stuff, and bound like a 'real' book. You are made to pay for one copy to place in the seminary library, and allowed to purchase other copies if you wish. I purchased a few extras and passed them out to a few selected people. While it's not a real book, nearly everyone acted like they were pleased to get a copy. To date, I can report that the copy in the James P. Boyce Library at The Southern Baptist Theological Seminary is still in pristine condition! I check on it every now and then. There's a good chance I've been the only person to touch it since it hit the shelf, with one exception. My friend Tom, who completed his degree right after I did, read the whole thing, and I know he stops for a quick look at each of our 'books' when he passes through Louisville. The only other person to persevere to the end of my book is my mom. She sounds pretty cool, doesn't she?

But for those who persevere in this book (a real one at last) and finish my story, I want to leave you with a lasting image of my mom and dad. This is the most important characteristic for you to know.

Both of them encouraged and supported me in telling this story. Read that again. It's not the book that they most want to brag about at work. I'm not sure they'll be very excited to purchase copies and hand them out. But we didn't have to cancel Thanksgiving. They didn't return my Christmas presents. No snide comments were lobbed. No angry phone calls or voicemails have been received. I don't recall the exact quotes but the spirit of their responses was gloriously similar. If God can use our story and you have the opportunity to tell it, then I think you should. In fact, you have the opportunity to read my dad's words as a conclusion to the book. It's rather hard to believe, isn't it?

To me it's not surprising because I know them both. This book may highlight one of the darkest periods in their lives, but it's not the period that defines them. If you want to know what does define them, it is the gospel of Jesus Christ.

They responded the way they did because God is faithful and they know it. He is faithful to forgive, to heal, to restore, and to renew. So after all of this detail, please know that they have been, by far, the largest shaping influence on my spiritual life. Despite a crooked journey, they still cling to the One who is able to save. He is still saving them; He is still saving me. And He will complete that work. At the convergence of these points – sin, grace, forgiveness, and healing – we find the sure and steady bedrock of hope.

As great as they are, though, my parents are not the bedrock of my story. More than the lasting image of them, I want to leave you with one other lasting thought: God's sovereign grace is the preventative medicine for the wounded soul. The praying, listening, sharing, confronting, and investing are critical instruments of grace. God's purpose is certain and it cannot be thwarted. But He is also a God of means. He ordains the end and He supplies the means.

Let's go back to Romans 8:

And we know that for those who love God all things work together for good, for those who are called according to his purpose. For those whom he foreknew he also predestined to be conformed to the image of his Son, in order that he might be the firstborn among many brothers. And those whom he predestined he also called, and those whom he called he also justified, and those whom he justified he also glorified. (8:28-30)

This passage contains what has been called the 'golden chain of salvation'. This chain begins with God's covenantal love before creation and extends into eternity. I quoted this passage back in chapter 5 to draw attention to the promise God gives to His people in the midst of suffering and trials. Here I want to zoom in on the ground for that promise. At the risk of glossing over it too quickly, notice the five actions God carries out for His people.

First, He foreknew us. While God has complete knowledge of future events, this word does not merely refer to information He had about us in the past. Instead, this teaches that God knew – intimately, lovingly knew – His people. Long before I was born, before I suffered, He knew more than just the statistics about my life: when I would be born, where I would live, how many hairs are on my head, etc. God knew the inmost secrets of my heart.

Second, He predestined us. That is, God marked me out beforehand. The comfort for the sufferer is that God, despite full knowledge of me, has chosen me. He set me apart for Himself and determined to do a work in me that I could never do for myself. My past, present, or future suffering cannot thwart what He has determined to do.

Third, He called us. He broke into my cold, dead heart with the light of the gospel. In calling me, He connects His eternal purpose for me with my experience. He not only informs me of His plan to save me, but He woos me to Himself. He called into the darkness of my sinful, rebellious heart and beckoned me out into His glorious light.

Fourth, He justified us. Justification is a legal or forensic term, belonging to the court of law. Paul explains justification in Romans 3 as at the heart of salvation. On the basis of faith in Jesus Christ, God justifies or declares the sinner to be righteous. He does not make the sinner perfect; instead, He reconciles the sinner to Himself on the basis of Jesus' work as the wrath-bearing substitute for sin. Again, God breaks down the dividing wall between us and brings us to Himself.

Fifth, He glorified us. This work of re-making us is yet in the future, but Paul uses a past tense verb to express it. The future work of God to complete His work in us is certain. God will glorify every single person He has foreknown, predestined, called, and justified. Philippians 1:6 states the promises even more clearly. 'And I am sure of this, that he who began a good work in you will bring it to completion at the day of Jesus Christ.'

The beauty of this chain for the sufferer lies in the certainty of God's past, present, and future work. This leads Paul to contend that believers are 'more than conquerors' in any and all situations because our God has begun this work that He is certain to finish.

While my parents pointed me to Christ in the midst of weakness, and my church family was an instrument of God's grace, His sovereignty has been my anchor. In this gospel, I have come to know the God who is holy, kind and sovereign. These bedrock truths form a sure foundation for my hope: so I do not hope in my parents, in the local church, or in my self-will or discipline. I do not hope in my wife or children, or in my theological training or ministry position. My hope is anchored to the promises of God for my future, that rest on the faithfulness of God in my past and present.

Let's go back once more to the summer of 1989. I was lying in the ditch, hurting, grieving, and reeling. But God had begun a good work in me and He has been faithful to continue it. This work is not unique to me. God did this work in Joseph in Egypt, and in the Roman believers in the first century. He's doing this work in the lives of our church members. As a pastor, these moments of crisis create opportunities for ministry. When the emotions are raw and the wounds are fresh, people often run to us for help. Don't forget that they need the gospel, for it is the power of God to save. Don't forget, healing takes a while and God's not in a hurry!

The last twenty-five years have been mostly ordinary. My parents did not reconcile their marriage; both eventually remarried, and our family expanded in a non-traditional way. Complete with step-parents and half-siblings, we found a new normal. We left the car in the ditch and moved on, so to speak. Despite a few quick, awkward conversations along the way, we didn't have long talks about the past crisis. We merged back onto the road in separate vehicles and kept going. When we're all together now for graduation ceremonies or birthday parties, the tension is mostly gone. Sometimes I wonder, though, if we've all found healing or if maybe we just learned to walk with a limp. I know for certain that God isn't finished with our healing because we are not yet glorified. Maybe this book will be another tool for His grace to us. And I pray it's an instrument of grace for you.

God's grace to me hasn't come through an earthquake, fire, or thunder and lightning. Instead, He keeps steadily transforming my heart and healing my hurt. Nobody really knew what to do or where to start back in 1989, but God did and He is faithful.

Afterword
Chris Carroll

Perhaps you were surprised when you read that the author of this book had given the pastor and father who failed him the privilege and honor of writing the last word of his book. However, it really wouldn't come as much of a surprise if you knew the author as I do. This book is both a testimony to God's faithfulness, and to a son's love and respect for his dad and mom. For those of you who know him personally, you know this speaks more to James's humility than anything else.

My 'one-word description of this little writing project' is still, 'awkward'. It is unavoidable since I'm confronted with my failures as a pastor and father in this book. It was many years after his sinful affair with Bathsheba that King David wrote, '… my sin is ever before me' (Ps. 51:3). It is true; my sin is ever before me because I failed. To repeat: I failed, and my heart still aches because of the deep hurt I caused a twelve-year-old, his older brother, and their mother. There were many friends and members of a loving church harmed by my failures as well and my heart aches for them too. I make no excuses for my sin, and I still live with some of the consequences in my life, but I handle them daily by faith in a compassionate and just God. James is accurate from the beginning of his book, when he writes:

> … but there had been smaller fissures along the way.
> … What I do know is that sin doesn't usually start big;
> it starts small and becomes big. I know that marriages
> don't often end because of a single disastrous moment.

What happened to our family did start small many years before, and it grew larger over a long period of time. Rehashing the details is something I did in many hours of counseling in the months following the divorce. It would serve no purpose to dig up bones long since buried. The scars are evident though, and as James indicated, we don't have long conversations about the distant past. With that being said, I have no doubt that one of my sins as the spiritual head of the household was my neglect of the small things. It is impossible to know the number of times I've thought about this in the past twenty-five-plus years. But, the one thing I do know is that my failure to trust and depend on God as a pastor, a father, and a husband was the result of my anger, bitterness, and pride. The biblical truth, 'Pride goes before destruction, and a haughty spirit before a fall' was evident in my life (Prov. 16:18). This allowed the *smaller fissures*, which caused all the pain you've read about in the pages of this book, to exist, grow, and damage the lives of those involved. Make no mistake, I'm not suggesting any of this excuses my sins. I made the sinful choices willfully and deliberately, and I cannot, and will not, point my finger at anyone except myself. I still live with the consequences of my sin, and I will always regret the hurt I caused.

Whether or not we realize it or admit it, the fact is that all sin causes harm to others. Sin is such a destructive force, and it always invades a person's life in subtle ways. It is much like an undetected cancer or deadly bacterial infection. When either goes undetected and untreated it spreads, causing death and destruction. There are many examples of sin in the Bible where the sin started in small, subtle, and unchecked ways. One of the saddest stories is when King David, a man after God's own heart, fell into sin and committed adultery with Bathsheba, the wife of Uriah. That would have been bad enough if that were the end of the story. But it's not, because David made things much worse when he discovered Bathsheba was pregnant. He set out to cover up his sin by ultimately having Uriah killed in battle. For some time, David lived thinking his sin was covered up, until God used the words of the faithful prophet named Nathan to confront him. Confessing his sin, he repented and humbled himself before God. Later, when David looked back on his experience, the evil of his sinful actions, his pride, the self-inflicting harm to himself, and the harm he caused others, he wrote Psalm

51, including the words, 'my sin is ever before me'. It's a beautiful prayer of confession for believers to pray when they want God to heal their wounds suffered because of their sin.

You may be in the midst of your hurt and suffering now. It may have been caused by another person's sin or your own sin. As a result, you feel alone, abandoned, without any hope. The Bible reminds you that you are not alone. It was the writer of Hebrews that reminded early Christians who were hurting and suffering that God is faithful in keeping His promise to them:

I will never leave you, nor forsake you. (Heb. 13:5)

In the midst of such hurting and suffering, and when the emotions are raw and the wounds are fresh, it is easy to feel abandoned by everyone, even God. Sin will certainly cause a person to feel this way whether it is the sin of another or their own. Regardless of the source of hurting and suffering, these are the crisis moments James reminds us are the opportunities for ministry.

The notion of writing such a book as this seemed so strange to me and, yes, awkward at first. I could only imagine someone ripping open a twenty-five-year-old wound that were scarred over, and pouring salt in that wound: painful, right?

I must confess the experience was painful, but it was also healing. Thank you James!

Dad.

Acknowledgments

Because the book is not a complete memoir, I tried to leave in the background as many details as I could about my life, and shine light on the gospel. In doing so, I largely omitted the person who knows my journey to healing better than anyone else, and who has been most instrumental along the way. She's wasn't there in 1989, but she's been my best friend for the last twenty-two-plus years. My wife, Mikila, deserves more credit than she'll ever receive for the role she continues to play in my spiritual development. She's also my favorite person in the world. I could never adequately thank her.

Outside my wife, my two favorite people on the planet are my children, Kenna and Jake. I fear they'll be severely disappointed at the end of this project because I'm pretty sure they think this book is going to become a bestseller. Though it's safely in the Lord's hands, I think their hopes are going to be dashed. I'm grateful to God for them, and grateful to them for their love. I hope someday they'll read this book and find the grace to forgive me for my failures. Lord knows, I'll need it.

I'm grateful for those who share this journey with me. To my mom, Toni, thank you for everything; the list is too long so I won't even try. Again, thanks, and hopefully you won't be the only person to read this one. I'm thankful to my dad, Chris, for humbly and graciously supporting and participating in this project. Not many men would do what you're doing and I'm grateful to God for you. Mark, we walked much of this road side-by-side and I'm thankful to have shared much of the journey with you. I'm proud to call you my brother and I pray this book will help you continue to heal, too.

To the saints of God at the First Baptist Church in Belfry, Kentucky, thank you. 'I thank my God in all my remembrance of you, always in every prayer of mine for you all making my prayer with joy, because of your partnership in the gospel from the first day until now' (Phil. 1:3-5). I mentioned a few of you in the pages and wish I could have listed you all. I praise God for you and your Christ-like love for me and my family. Only God knew how much He could accomplish inside that inconspicuous little church deep in the mountains of eastern Kentucky. Your place in the world may seem insignificant, but your role in my life was anything but. Thank you and keep pressing on.

Finally, a few of my friends deserve thanks for helping to bring this book to reality. Thanks to Brian Croft for getting it rolling and bringing it home. He's a faithful brother and dear friend. I look forward to laboring together in the future. To my friend and personal editor, Ed Hardin, I'm sorry and thanks. You deserve more credit for the finished product than a couple of sentences on one of the last pages, but that's how it goes. To Ms Marcella, I appreciate your help very much. Your editing contributions, encouragement, and support mean the world to me. Thanks to my family at Parkway Baptist Church for persevering with me as their pastor, as I am still very much being sanctified. We'll get there someday.

M E A
CULPA

LEARNING FROM MISTAKES
IN THE MINISTRY

KYLE MᶜCLELLAN

Mea Culpa
by Kyle McClellan

From the Foreword by Brian Croft: Kyle McClellan has gone into a church "with guns blazing" and he was quickly fired. He has experienced the disappointment of unmet expectations and left because of this. He has pastored a destructive church that chewed him up and spat him out. He has felt the pull of the bigger and better church trying to woo him away. He has faced the burnout and fatigue that many pastors experience that causes them to bail. Read this book. Learn from him. Receive the essential lessons from a wise, broken man who has lived it, possesses the scars from it, owns the T-shirt and yet by the grace of God still stands.

ISBN: 978-1-78191-529-5

Christian Focus Publications

Our mission statement –

STAYING FAITHFUL

In dependence upon God we seek to impact the world through literature faithful to His infallible Word, the Bible. Our aim is to ensure that the Lord Jesus Christ is presented as the only hope to obtain forgiveness of sin, live a useful life and look forward to heaven with Him.

Our books are published in four imprints:

CHRISTIAN FOCUS

Popular works including biographies, commentaries, basic doc-trine and Christian living.

CHRISTIAN HERITAGE

Books representing some of the best material from the rich heritage of the church.

MENTOR

Books written at a level suitable for Bible College and seminary students, pastors, and other serious readers. The imprint includes commentaries, doctrinal studies, examination of current issues and church history.

CF4•K

Children's books for quality Bible teaching and for all age groups: Sunday school curriculum, puzzle and activity books; personal and family devotional titles, biographies and inspirational stories – because you are never too young to know Jesus!

Christian Focus Publications Ltd,
Geanies House, Fearn, Ross-shire,
IV20 1TW, Scotland, United Kingdom.
www.christianfocus.com